AMARONE

*The Making of an Italian
Wine Phenomenon*

Other Regional Reference Books From
THE WINE APPRECIATION GUILD
"The Best Wine Book Publisher in the US."
—Edward Cointreau, Gourmand World Cookbook Award

Africa Uncorked, John and Erica Platter (ISBN 1-891267-52-3)

Armagnac, Charles Neal (ISBN 1-891267-20-5)

Atlas of Italian Spumanti, Zanfi (ISBN 978-8-864030-36-4)

Calvados, Neal (ISBN 978-0-615-44640-0)

Chancers & Visionaries, Stewart (ISBN 978-1-869620-70-7)

Chilean Wine Heritage, Rodrigo Alvarado (ISBN 1-891267-80-9)

Chow! Venice, Shannon Essa and Ruth Edenbaum (ISBN 1-934259-00-4)

Encyclopedia of American Wine, William I. Kaurman (ISBN 0-932664-39-3)

Essential Guide to South African Wine, 2nd Ed., Elmari Swart (ISBN 978-0-980274-23-0)

Garden State Wineries Guide, Jackson (ISBN 978-1-934259-57-3)

Ghost Wineries of the Napa Valley, Irene Whitford Haynes (ISBN 0-932664-90-3)

The Global Encyclopedia of Wine, Edited by Peter Forrestal (ISBN 1-891267-38-8)

Good Wine, Bad Language, Great Vineyards: Australia (ISBN 0977514722)

Good Wine, Bad Language, Great Vineyards: New Zealand (ISBN 0-977514-72-2)

Grands Crus of Bordeaux, Hans Walraven (ISBN 0-932664-94-6)

Grape Man of Texas, McLeRoy and Renfro (ISBN 1-934259-04-7)

Hospice de Beaune, Gotti (ISBN 978-2-35-156-049-5)

How to Import Wine, Gray (ISBN 978-1-934259-61-0)

Hungary, David Copp (ISBN 963-86759-6-9)

I Supertuscan, Carlo Gambi (ISBN 88-88482-40-7)

Journey Among the Great Wines of Sicily, Carlo Gambi (ISBN 88-88482-10-5)

Lombardia, Zanfi (ISBN 978-8-888482-98-9)

Napa Wine: A History, Charles L. Sullivan (ISBN 1-891267-07-8)

The New Italy, Daniele Cernelli and Marco Sabellico (ISBN 1-891267-32-9)

New Wines of Spain, Tony Lord (ISBN 0-932664-59-8)

Oregon Eco-Friendly Wine, Clive Michelsen (ISBN 91-975326-4-9)

The Origins of Chilean Wine, Hernandez (ISBN 978-956316-082-6)

Piedmont, Carlo Gambi (ISBN 88-88482-43-1

Pinot Noir, A New Zealand Story, Saker (ISBN 978-1-86979-279-4))

Pleasures of the Canary Islands, Ann and Larry Walker (ISBN 0-932664-75-X)

Pocket Encyclopedia of American Wine, Northwest, William I. Kaufman (ISBN 0-932664-58-X)

Pocket Encyclopedia of California Wine, William I. Kaufman (ISBN 0-932664-42-3)

Portugal's Wines & Wine Makers, New Revised Edition, Richard Mason (ISBN 1-891267-01-9)

Rich,Rare & Red, Ben Howkins (ISBN 1-891267-63-9)

Sauternes, Jeffrey Benson and Alastair McKenzie (ISBN 0-856673-60-9)

Tokaj, David Copp (ISBN 963-87524-3-2)

Tokaji Wine, Lambert-Gocs (ISBN 978-1-934259-49-8)

Top 100 South African Wines, von Holdt (ISBN 978-098027-425-7)

Tuscany, Zanfi (ISBN 9788864030050)

Veneto, Zanfi (ISBN 978-8-888482-80-4)

What Price Bordeaux , Lewin (ISBN 978-1-934-25-9)

White Burgundy, Christopher Fielden (ISBN 0-932664-62-8)

The Wines of Baja California, Ralph Amey (ISBN 1-891267-65-5)

The Wines of France, Clive Coates (ISBN 1-891267-14-0)

AMARONE

*The Making of an Italian
Wine Phenomenon*

KATE SINGLETON

The Wine Appreciation Guild
San Francisco

Amarone
The making of an Italian wine phenomenon

The Wine Appreciation Guild
360 Swift Avenue
South San Francisco, CA 94080
(650) 866-3020
www.wineappreciation.com

ISBN: 978-1-935879-82-4

Printed in China

CONTENTS

For their help, patience and friendship, I am greatly indebted to Dora Stopazzolo, Cristina Valenza, Elisabetta Tollapi, Raffaele Boscaini and Andrea Dal Cin. Grazie mille!

FOREWORD

I was born in the Valpolicella and identify with the land of Amarone. To understand what Amarone really represents you have to have been born here into a family of winegrowers, surrounded by these gentle hillsides. Amarone is more than just a wine or a technique—it's a philosophy, an art, a life companion. I was born in one of the typical three-story houses; actually, they had four floors if you count the vaulted underground cellar. In such houses the family lived by day on the ground floor, and slept above on the first floor, sandwiched between the grapes quietly drying on trays in the attic and the cellar, where all the rites of fermentation and aging took place. Only someone who has lived this closely with the grapes and the wine can know what Amarone signifies-what it means to select the bunches for drying, to lay them out on cane trays, to stack them up in the drying lofts and keep them under constant observation, as you would a family member whose well-being is particularly dear to you. And not for just a day or two, but for months-from the end of September through to February, when the grapes are ready for crushing. As children we would wake up early in the morning as the farmhands padded quietly up the stairs to place the wrinkled bunches into copper buckets, which they then took down to the cellar. They went barefoot so that they didn't dirty the floors. Down below, the cellar door was kept closed to stop the winter cold from hindering fermentation. The grapes were crushed with hand-operated rollers, and the must was transferred to the fermentation vats in shoulder-held conical containers. Everything was done by hand, in a time-honored series of measured actions, under the vigilant supervision of my father. The other person who kept an eye on the whole process was my aunt Toscana, who invited the workers up for a break in the sitting room above, because "you must never eat bread in the cellar." That applied to us children as well, though I have never quite understood exactly why . . .

In houses like ours you breathed the scents of the Amarone grapes, and I still have distinct memories of how the intense cherry fragrance of the fresh grapes was gradually transformed into the quietly sweet smell of semi-dried grapes. The turning point for us children was Saint Lucy's Day, at the beginning of December, when another scent pervaded the house: that of oranges, still slightly unripe but already fragrant. The Saint used to leave them as gifts at the foot of our beds.

During those months, the original smell of grapes gave way to other odors that arose from the cellar. At first, it was the penetrating sweetness of crushed grapes, then the acrid pungency of fermentation, followed by the austere aroma of wood and wine that would be ready for drinking by the beginning of summer. For us children, and I believe for the adults too, trying to guess from the smell what the weather was going to be like that day became a kind of game. Different smells came to the fore when the atmospheric pressure was low, and others when it was high. "Upstairs" as opposed to "downstairs" odors. But before checking the sky we used to consult a country calendar known as "Pojana maggiore," which hung from a hook on the kitchen door. It showed the phases of the moon and offered a weather forecast of its own. That done, we were finally ready to open the window and find out who had won.

As children we weren't supposed to go up into the drying loft. Sergio and I did, of course, drawn not only by the scents but also by the wonderful colors of the grapes that turned from deep red to mauve. Of course we had to sample them, our favorites being the ones that had tiny white dots on them. These were the creamiest and the sweetest, extraordinarily intense in their over-ripeness, almost like loquats. I only realized later that we were appreciating the magic of noble rot. My other younger brothers, Bruno and Mario, were born too late to have enjoyed these experiences!

Things began to change in the mid-1950s, and have undergone radical transformation over the past several decades. What was once a poetic act of love has necessarily become a business. Like the best of products made in Italy, however, premium Amarone still requires the witting collaboration of hands, head and heart. Alas, not every Amarone is worthy of the name.

At present there are over two hundred Amarone labels on the market. Some of them are products of unquestionable quality; others will end up on supermarket shelves and embody little or nothing of the glory of this ancient, noble wine. Such exponential growth corresponds to a marked increase in the number of producers, many of whom have jumped on the bandwagon of the wine's worldwide acclaim. Wineries of this sort consider Amarone a business opportunity, another way of making money. There are only a dozen or so historic wineries who have Amarone in their DNA, who have devoted their lifeblood to quality production, struggling to make their presence felt on a market that was not initially well disposed towards a wine deemed unfashionable, provincial and rustic. From the grape varieties involved to the production techniques, Amarone failed to fit in with the canons of modern enology.

I have many memories of taking important wine critics and journalists around our cellars, watching them taste the wine, then hearing them say with a condescending smile, "I'm not saying it isn't a good wine, and of course it's important for you and your birthplace, but believe me, if you want to get your foot into the international market, consider planting Cabernet and Merlot . . ."

In the first edition of his *Wine Companion*, even Hugh Johnson, that most refined and attentive of critics, declared that "at any Veronese gathering the last bottle to be served is Recioto either in its sweet form or in its powerful, dry, velvety but astringent and bitter Amarone." There's a suggestion here that the wine is somehow unbalanced, and that its local aficionados are too provincial to know any better. He concludes the entry with some advice: "... keep a glass of youthful Valpolicella to hand to quench your thirst!"

In actual fact Hugh Johnson had a point. The Amarones he refers to predate the early 1980s, when we at Masi started introducing technical improvements that were to change the profile of the wine, introducing it to a much wider audience and paving the way for its current success. Sometimes an individual can change dramatically in order to please the person he or she loves. Something similar happened between us and Amarone: we really thought about it, took stock of its shortcomings, and felt passionate enough about it to bring about change. Amarone is a symbol of everything we stand for; it's part of our heritage and something we're hugely proud of, so we have put everything possible into making sure it survived the difficult years.

In recollecting those distant times when I first became aware of my deep affection for the wine, I simply wish to illustrate one aspect of a life devoted to the study, production, tasting and discussion of Amarone. Its technical evolution and the widespread acclaim that came in its wake are part of the same process. I have promoted Amarone with great pride, as one would a precious family treasure, conscious that I was introducing the wider world to one of the most significant symbols of Verona and the Veneto. Granted, there are plenty of others, including the gondola and the domes of San Marco in Venice, and the Arena or Juliet's balcony in Verona. The difference is, of course, that Amarone is a symbol that can be transported, translated and transferred. I have travelled with it across the five continents, introducing it to myriad different consumers who have unfailingly gratified my efforts with surprise, curiosity and a positive verdict.

Many countries had no experience of Amarone before I took it there. Sweden is a case in point: the State Monopoly had never listed an Amarone before the mid-1980s, when I persuaded them to take the first 240 bottles of Vaio Armaron

Serego Alighieri. Today the discerning Swedish market welcomes Amarone with open arms.

On account of my itinerant passion and conviction, I have often been called "Mr. Amarone" by both the international press and by people who have taken part in the hundreds of thematic tasting sessions organized across the globe. It's a nickname I like and am proud of, because it makes me feel like a miniature Marco Polo, intrigued by the discovery of new cultures, but also aware of introducing something of my own culture as an Italian, and more specifically as a *Veneto*, and indeed a *Valpolicellese*.

I do have one small regret, however: that I never managed to persuade my wife to become actively involved in my adventure with Amarone. Outside the family, the focus of Giuliana's talent has always been her painting, which she's very good at. I greatly appreciate that she has accepted my peripatetic existence without making me feel guilty. It is probably due to her wisdom that we still have so much to share, including our three splendid children and their young families.

There are multiple threads to the story of my involvement in the wine business. In a number of long, enjoyable conversations, I have tried to disentangle them for my friend Kate Singleton, who has woven together my own personal story, that of my family and the land I come from with the history of the wine, the way it is made and what it stands for. Her mixture of sensitivity and professional skill have also allowed her to work my emotional attachment into the overall fabric of the book, and for this I am especially grateful.

Sandro Boscaini
Gargagnago, 29 November 2010

I

PRELUDE

nce upon a time, though not so very long ago, in the heart of Milan there was a large, smoky tavern in a little side street off the central Via Meravigli. The Osteria Trani was largely patronized by bibulous locals, but in the evenings the customers often included a group of students. One of these was Sandro Boscaini, whose daytime pursuit was a Bachelor's degree at the Università Cattolica just around the corner.

"In those days the patrons of the Osteria Trani could choose between wines described as *vin ciar*, *vin scur* and *vin gross*," Sandro recalls. "The last of these was a robust red from Sicily or Apulia, sun-baked southern regions that typically produce wines of great strength, often used for blending. The *vin scur*, or dark wine, on the other hand, was a classic, deep ruby red from Piedmont. As for the *vin ciar*, it was a lighter red made from vines grown on the temperate hillsides of the Valpolicella, near Verona. This is where I come from. It's an area of great natural beauty long devoted to viticulture."

The Boscaini family were established winemakers. Sandro's father, Guido, used to travel up to Milan every Friday to conclude deals, arrange supplies for the city and harass the agents who covered neighboring towns such as Novara, Vercelli, Como and Varese. These negotiations took place by the Borsa, or stock exchange, a handsome neoclassical building just behind Piazza dei Mercanti. At lunchtime, a vociferous contingent of wine merchants from the Veneto would entirely take over the Mercanti restaurant, located under the portico overlooking the market square. Verona, their hometown, was a center for winemaking and had an important and more discerning wine market of its own. Milan, however, was already to some extent an international city, and thus an essential interface for trade, especially towards Switzerland and northern Europe.

All that was fifty or so years ago. Much has changed in the meantime. Although Milan remains Italy's foremost hub for business, today Verona has taken over as the country's pre-eminent wine market. This is not so much because an annual output of just over 678 million liters places the Veneto among Italy's most prolific wine-producing regions, but because the people of the area have a particular gift for commerce: they've been perfecting it for some 800 years, since the glorious days of the Most Serene Republic of Venice, when Venetian merchants dominated the lucrative timber, spice and silk trades. Today Verona hosts both Italy's most important exchange in bulk wines, and Vinitaly, the world's foremost wine fair. Moreover, it handles much of the commercialization and distribution of the country's superior bottled wines.

Prominent among those superior products are wines made in the Valpolicella itself. The district comprises three gentle valleys overlooking Verona and Lake Garda from the northeast. Terraces supported by dry stone walls known as *marogne* are a typical feature of the land devoted to viticulture, with further walls delimiting the properties. Winter climates are mild, thanks to sunlight reflected from the lake. Omnipresent cherry trees create clouds of pink and white blossom in spring, while fresh breezes mitigate the heat of summer. Stretching languidly down from the Lessini Mountains to the River Adige, the sunny hillsides and rocky canyons of the Valpolicella have largely escaped the ravages of modernity.

Viticulture on these hillsides has always been a way of life. Fossilized remains found locally testify to the existence of cultivated vines of the *Vitis vinifera sativa* species dating back to the Iron Age. The Arusnati, the early inhabitants of the Valpolicella, were certainly winemakers. By the second century B.C.E., the wine they produced had gained a name for itself as far afield as Rome. The historian Suetonius declared that the Emperor Augustus, who was known for his temperance, made an exception when it came to wines from the Valpolicella: "... *maxime delectatus est Raetico*," the delectability pertaining to the wines of the Rhaetians, the term used by the Romans to refer to the people of the Verona area.

It is only in relatively recent years, however, that wines made from grapes grown on the mineral-rich soils of the Valpolicella have won acclaim throughout the wine-drinking world. The key to this success has been the ability of a few wineries in exalting the quality and individuality of their most prestigious product, Amarone, a rich, complex, dry red based on three indigenous grape varieties that are dried before crushing. Just one of many recent testimonials speaks chapters for the extent of this acclaim. At the 2009 edition of the prestigious London-based International Wine Challenge, a single wine from the Valpolicella carried off the trophies for the best Italian red, the best Venetian red and the best Amarone.

That particular wine was the Campolongo di Torbe 2004, an Amarone produced by the Masi winery, headed by Sandro Boscaini. The triple accolade is interesting, in that it recognizes the excellence of a type of wine that has not always earned the critics' unqualified praise. For many years Amarone was considered unbalanced, heavy, and somewhat awkward: a dried grape wine, but not a dessert wine; a "meditation wine," which sounded worthy but seemed to distract the focus from the pleasure of actual drinking. Even at its best, Amarone failed to tally with the taste parameters of wine writers brought up on international varietals.

The Masi winery has been a major agent of this change, in both the product and people's perception of it. It has refined production methods, introduced new wines made with traditional varieties and techniques, and persuaded critics to expand their palates. As a result, the wines have long done exceptionally well at a variety of tasting events, winning double the number of 90+ scores with *Wine Spectator* than their closest competitors.

To have transformed Veronese wines from the *vin ciar* of student libations to a number of award-winning Amarones is a remarkable achievement that marries foresight with tradition. Devotion to the vineyard has gone hand in hand with technical improvements and growing awareness of an evolving market. Over one-and-a-half centuries have gone into the development of this multi-faceted approach.

The Boscainis have long been involved in winemaking in the Valpolicella, certainly since 1772, when the family acquired through marriage the Vaio di Masi vineyard (*vaio* means valley in the local dialect), from which the current winery derives its name.

For three generations the family winery revolved around the original property, located high up near the village of Torbe, which straddles the Marano and Negrar Valleys. Then, in 1882, Sandro's grandfather, Paolo, and his brother, Battista, purchased two substantial properties lower down the Marano Valley, in the Valgatara district. At this point the cellars and offices of what was to become Boscaini Paolo e figli were relocated to the new acquisition, which to this day still houses the main winemaking facility with its various modern extensions.

Since then the estate has been gradually and selectively extended to comprise vineyards in all the prime growing areas. Sandro's father, Guido, continued to acquire land he deemed suitable for viticulture, some of it in the Soave and the Bardolino areas to the east and west of the Valpolicella. The trend has continued up to the present, with the Masi estate currently comprising 560 hectares of vineyard and controlling the output of a further 580.

In its recognition of the importance of micro-zones for the production of distinctive wines, the family was ahead of its time. The fact that they were not only growers and winemakers, but also wine merchants, was an advantage. They understood the local market, and had the vision to imagine how it might be expanded in the future.

This attention to commerce is typical of the people of the region. "It's in our DNA," Sandro declares. "I believe the Veneti have a certain creative flair. We're from the terra firma, so we're involved in production. But we're also merchants. We like to sell the products of our land."

Sandro's particular mixture of energy and perspicacity is accompanied by a pleasant, open manner, an eye for quality and a quiet sense of humor. Whether these are peculiarly Venetian qualities is open to debate. What is clear, however, is the way the *cultura veneta*, or the heritage of the Veneto, inspires his vitality and vision. Thirty years ago it led to the creation of the Masi Prize for Venetian Civilization, and thereafter to what has become one of the most important institutes for the promotion of the Venetian cultural heritage, the Masi Foundation.

A glance at Masi's more recent acquisitions reveals two themes that are particularly close to Sandro's heart: anything, especially wine, that is an expression of Venetian values; and the promise of *appassimento*, the winemaking technique based on the winter fermentation of dried grapes that is essential to Amarone, but is also applicable to other dry wines. Belief in the value of appassimento has led Masi to experiment with grape varieties much further afield. The products of the Tupungato winery at Mendoza in Argentina, one of Masi's more recent investments, have amply vindicated this conviction.

What Sandro Boscaini relates to in terms of the Venetian heritage goes well beyond the confines of the present-day Region of the Veneto, an administrative more than a geographical entity that only dates back a little over one hundred years. The Venetian Republic, which preceded it by five centuries, stretched north and northeast into the Val d'Adige and Friuli, comprising cities such as Udine and Rovereto. This much wider area shares not only aspects of dialect, but also traits that characterized Venice at the height of its powers, among them a methodical approach, a sense of purpose, flair for innovation and an appreciation of measured elegance.

"For years I've nurtured this dream of helping revive the nobility of winemaking in the wider area that once came under the aegis of Venice," Sandro declares. "Unlike other wine producing regions such as Tuscany, where there was never much industry, the Veneto witnessed a rapid increase in the availability of factory jobs in the late twentieth century. This hastened the demise of share-crop farming, leading to a scarcity of laborers for the great patrician estates. While some landowners struggled on with grape growing, many gave up on labor-intensive cultivation and sold off portions of their land." Their predicament was an opportunity for a mutually beneficial joint venture. Masi would provide the knowhow, including the commercial network, and the aristocratic families would supply the land and the blazoned history. The first such collaboration regarded the Serego Alighieri estate in the Valpolicella. Later came the Bossi Fedrigotti winery at Rovereto in the Trentino. Since then, the winery has also invested in vineyards in neighboring Friuli.

"History is a heritage, but not a straitjacket. Everyone has *terroir*. But what we have here in the Valpolicella is an age-old technique that is unique to the area. Appassimento in the production of dry wines is a process we have come to understand in considerable depth. Its potential for enhancing both red and white wines is remarkable. In Piedmont, they've been making Barolo for 300 years, and they never think of doing anything different. We Veneti can't stop ourselves studying processes that could lead to innovation."

Past and Present

A great deal has changed in winemaking in the Valpolicella since Sandro first played a role in the family winery. He would actually insist that he has been involved in the business since he was a youngster, simply because wine was the subject of most mealtime conversations when he was a child. "That was what the whole family talked about," he recalls.

At the time, commerce in wine in Italy was still in its infancy. What happened at the Boscaini winery would have been fairly typical: buyers visited the cellars, often accompanied by an intermediary, and sampled from the various casks, chalking their signature on the barrel of their choice. Once this selection had been established, everyone adjourned for a handsome lunch prepared in the family home by Sandro's mother. A few days later the casks were loaded onto a truck, delivered to their various destinations, and the empties were taken back to the winery ready for the next vintage. Apart from the modernization of the transport, little had changed in generations.

As with any form of agriculture, there were moments beset with worry. Apart from bad harvests and fluctuating prices, there was also the onset of unscrupulous competition on the part of companies that bought up bulk wines from other regions, which they blended and sold for local. There were hard times as well as good ones.

Perhaps it was one of those periodical crises in the wine trade that persuaded Guido Boscaini to suggest that Sandro, the oldest of his four sons, should study to become a pharmacist or a notary. The boy's interests lay in the humanities, however, and after finishing his secondary education at the Liceo Classico in Verona he opted to study for a degree in economics and business administration at the University in Milan. It was an honorable compromise, allowing him to focus on the historical aspects of his subject and to accompany his father on those Friday visits when there were agents to meet, prices to be discussed and supplies to be arranged.

When the time came to work on his thesis, Sandro found he was in a position to return to the world of wine. The government had asked the Milan-based Unione Italiana Vini to undertake a survey of the incipient risks of monopolies in the wine business. A group of wine merchants had founded this institution back in 1895, with the aim of fighting duties on agricultural products, combatting fraudulent practices, and providing services for the development of the wine trade. It was a mine of information, to which Sandro turned for his study of the history of the distribution of Italian wines.

In the early months of 1964, just as he was completing his research, the chairman of the Fiera di Verona contacted the director of the Unione Italiana Vini to ask for advice. In those days

Verona hosted three fairs a year, including an Agriculture Fair held in March. At this event, the most important of its sort in Europe, there were two pavilions devoted to viticulture. With the advent of massive modern agricultural machinery, however, most visitors rushed to admire the spectacular combine harvesters and giant tractors and largely neglected the winemakers in Pavilions 40 and 41. In the face of such competition, it seemed pointless to try to lure people where they were less inclined to go. Instead, it was proposed that Verona should hold a fair entirely devoted to wine. The director of the Unione Italiana Vini informed his colleagues in Verona that he had a young man studying in his archives who would be just the person to work on such a project.

Sandro was signed up for a one-year contract back in Verona in the early months of 1964, before he had even completed his degree. "It was a fascinating experience," he recalls. "It gave me the chance to get to know people from all over the country, and to go to Rome to follow up what I had in mind. It all broadened my outlook enormously."

His aim was to formulate proposals that would help shape Vinitaly, Verona's major wine fair. Central to his ideas was the recognition that wine required the kind of promotion that can engage the non-specialist public. While this is self-evident today, fifty years ago it implied some innovative thinking, since the prospect of export was beyond most people's horizons. Sandro suggested that a wine fair held just before Christmas would encourage consumers to think of wine as a possible seasonal gift. He also believed that holding a wine fair in the spring, before the start of the summer tourist season, would allow producers to showcase their wines to restaurateurs, hoteliers and their international clientele. The third proposal revolved around the conviction that an event of this sort should bring together specialist debate and exchange of ideas. The Masi international seminars that are key features of Vinitaly today are the logical development of this concept.

The job with the Fiera lasted for nearly two years. The first two editions of the new Wine Fair were called "*Le giornate del vino italiano*" (Italian Wine Days), and comprised both a display of wines and opportunities for tasting. Twenty or so exhibitors took part, one of them being Boscaini Paolo e figli, the family winery. Sandro reckons that he is probably the only person to have attended Vinitaly constantly since its inception.

To see his oldest son successfully involved in the wider world of wine must ultimately have been gratifying for Signor Boscaini senior, whatever his earlier misgivings might have been. Furthermore, Guido's second-born, Sergio, was busy completing his studies in enology at the prestigious Institute of Viticulture in the neighboring town of Conegliano, and there were four cousins likely to be joining the family enterprise in the coming years. Perhaps Sandro could be persuaded to come on board as well. Guido broached the subject during his son's last months at the Fiera.

Apart from a range of basic wines, at the time the Boscaini winery was producing a special selection of Recioto, the traditional sweet dessert wine; an Amarone; and the lighter, elegant Valpolicella Classico under the Tenuta dei Masi label. These superior products largely went to a few carefully selected restaurants in Verona and the main cities of northern Italy. In working with the family business, Sandro saw that he would also have the opportunity to bring a dream project to fruition: to turn the Tenuta dei Masi into a niche winery that reflected the most historic family vineyards. Guido agreed. He had great faith in his sons, recognizing that their education and travel had probably given them better tools for anticipating future market trends.

A law instituting recognized appellations, known as DOCs, was passed in 1963, and became effective in 1965. Sandro's work at the Fiera had given him an insider's picture of the promise and shortcomings of Italian viticulture, and he was greatly in favor of the new legislation, convinced that the Denominazione di Origine Controllata (denomination of controlled origin) would focus consumers' interests on particular growing areas, thereby counteracting the stranglehold of a small number of large wine concerns that cared little for growers but had the commercial clout to shape the market in their own image.

"I was full of youthful optimism and considerable naïveté. In my degree thesis I had argued that the establishment of DOCs would help the different micro-zones devoted to quality winemaking outshine individual labels. That is something I now completely reject, both as a concept and in terms of historical experience. Rather than embrace a collective value, unfortunately there will always be a few winemakers who think they can get away with short cuts, and that ruins the situation for the honest majority. But even the way the rules are drawn up is often so ambiguous that it's asking for trouble. For example, when the Valpolcella DOC was finally recognized in 1968, it already showed signs of the sort of compromise that has beleaguered the whole system. The established growing areas were extended to include the Valpantena and beyond, where soils, microclimate and elevation are quite different. Granted, the designation 'Classico' was reserved for the products of the original growing area, but there was a general lack of clarity on the part of the Consortium of producers. I felt this was counterproductive, and it was certainly confusing for consumers."

By the end of the 1970s, Sandro was so disgruntled by the behavior of the Consortium that he decided to resign from it. Since then, Italy has seen the affirmation of certain DOCs, especially in regions such as Tuscany, where the landscape has become an icon that enhances the perception of quality. In other areas, however, a number of dubious DOCs have also been introduced, largely at the behest of some local politician more interested in gaining votes than furthering excellence in wine production. And even within some of the established appellations there have been concessions in terms of yield and grape variety that are unlikely to contribute to quality. Sandro shrugs his shoulders at such myopic developments, having long moved on to more fruitful convictions. "The truth is," he says, "that it's particular labels that open up markets for a whole growing area. Brands forge ahead, bringing viticultural micro-zones in their wake."

As far as the Veneto was concerned, a few major wine concerns were flooding the market with products of mixed provenance that had little to do with local grape varieties or production methods. Around Verona, for example, important wineries such as Bolla, Castagna, Peternella and Ruffo changed the focus of investment from the vineyard to cellar technology and commercial structure. In other words, they considered themselves more industrialists than winemakers. "It was as though vineyards had become just an option for wineries," Sandro recalls. "Of course tending vineyards properly is expensive and requires a lot of labor. But that's what we were all about. The wine industrialists laughed at us, dismissing us as a bunch of backward-looking bumpkins. But we were actually on the right track because we really did represent the land, which is a concept to which some of them have had to return in order to survive. Though the wine industry dominated the market at the time, it was insensitive to the nascent demand for quality linked to local provenance, to roots. This was its undoing."

Sandro decided to stake out the challenge in terms of quality. His idea was to create an Amarone under the Masi label that would become a new paradigm for this type of wine, a product that spoke clearly to an increasingly discerning consumer.

To this end, in 1966 he called in a skilled winemaker who had suffered a major setback. Nino Franceschetti was originally involved with the S. Sofia estate, a Valpolicella winery that had initially shown great promise, but had collapsed through poor management. Sandro had observed this trajectory with interest. Housed in a magnificent Palladian villa, the winery had believed in *terroir*, in using grapes from carefully tended vineyards belonging to the estate, but had over-stretched itself financially. There was a lesson to be learnt here: respect for the local heritage was essential, and employing a first rate enologist was commendable, but streamlined cellars and all-out promotion could wait.

Guido agreed with Sandro's view of this experience. Yet both appreciated that acquiring more space and a well-positioned headquarters for the Tenuta dei Masi project could end up by benefitting the entire family business. The right opportunity arose when the patrician Serego Alighieri family, whose neighboring vineyards produced grapes for the Boscaini winery, decided to sell a pleasant Art Nouveau villa with its own small cellars in the village of Gargagnago, a few miles from the Valgatara winery.

The new facility would provide space for a selection of superior wines, with Amarone at the top. The differentiation was underscored on the label with the name of the new company: *Azienda Agricola Masi, proprietà Boscaini Paolo e figli*, surrounded by an eighteenth century decorative motif Sandro had found sorting through the family business archive, complete with the motto "*Nectar angelorum hominibus.*" It was a sort of declaration of how past, present and future could go hand in hand.

Launching Masi

The first vintages on the market did so well that the family decided to separate Masi as a company from the Boscaini concern. "We had credibility because we were winegrowers, and to this we were able to add image, which we acquired through two products in particular," Sandro explains. "One was the Amarone, which had an aura of its own, partly because it was still a relatively rare wine. It takes many years and great skill to make a good Amarone, so most wineries preferred to focus on the far simpler Valpolicella. The other Masi wine that made a huge impact from its first appearance was really the fruit of an idea my father had been working on since 1958. He had the vision to see that the market would embrace a wine that was lighter than an Amarone, which is made from dried grapes, yet had more depth than the Valpolicella, which is an immediately drinkable, lighter wine. Since both are made from the same grape varieties, my father felt it should be possible to marry freshness with depth of color and aroma by re-fermenting the lighter wine on the skins of the Amarone. The idea was inspired by what in Tuscany used to go by the name of *governo*, meaning the addition of slightly dried grapes to young wines to obtain further fermentation and greater body in the end product. Here in the Veneto there was also the old country practice of making *vinello*, a weak everyday wine, by adding water to fermented grape skins."

The process involved making the wine in March, once the Amarone had been racked to remove it from the gross lees. Adding the fresh wine to these skins naturally engendered a secondary fermentation that continued for around fifteen to twenty days. After several years of trials and comparisons, the Boscainis felt they had perfected the technique, and in 1967 they launched the 1964 vintage, calling it "Campofiorin Ripasso," a name that they later registered as a trademark.

The new release was an immediate success, appealing to the discerning public at home and abroad, and attracting the attention of many critics who had hitherto given short shrift to the wines of the Valpolicella. Burton Anderson described it as "a table wine of luxuriant size and complexity . . ., the prototype for the new-style Veronese red."

In the following years, ripples from Masi's small enological revolution touched practically every prominent winery of the area. Not all the emulators were respectful of the trademark, however, and the name *Ripasso* (literally, passed over twice), turned up on a variety of labels. Rather than contest his competitors over this appropriation, Sandro Boscaini decided to donate the trademark to the Verona Chamber of Commerce. There seemed to be no point in creating antagonism when the Valpolicella at large stood to benefit from the innovation-to add to which, in the meantime Masi had moved on to an improved version of the technique, consisting of double fermentation.

Aided by Nino Franceschetti, the Boscainis had come to understand that grape skins impart their finer tannins to the first wine, reserving for the second brew a degree of asperity that was at odds with what they had in mind. So in the early 1980s they changed tack, replacing the Amarone lees with uncrushed semi-dried grapes to effect a much shorter second fermentation in November. Around twelve days, they discovered, was time enough to invest the fruity young wine with greater aromatic concentration and a more rounded tannic structure: Campofiorin had taken over from *ripasso*.

Popular Canadian food and drink commentator Jurgen Gothe has described the Ripasso as "a remarkable creation with the lightness of Valpolicella and the intensity of Amarone." His countryman Tony Aspler was won over by this "Valpolicella with attitude." As for British wine writer and critic Hugh Johnson, he praised Masi for its devotion to "unerring selection and ingenious techniques."[1] Today there is hardly an estate in the area that does not produce its own version of what Monica Larner recently praised in *Wine Enthusiast* as "an ingenious hybrid of two historic reds from the Veneto, one of the hottest new wines to emerge from Italy."[2]

From the outset, the success of Campofiorin was based on three traits typical of the Masi winery: great care in grape growing; an ability to think creatively; and a prescient understanding of what the market was ready for. The same characteristics also underlie Sandro Boscaini's flagship accomplishment, the renewal of Amarone, in both substance and image. When he took the Tenuta dei Masi in hand, Amarone was a bit like an elderly General renowned for his fortitude, but indulgent at home: full of magnificent memories, but also given to forgetfulness; proud in stance, but a bit wobbly on the legs. At its best, it was very good, but more often than not it revealed imbalances that were hard to ignore.

The problem lay in the winter fermentation of dried grapes of the traditional Corvina, Rondinella and Molinara varieties. Because the yeasts involved in transforming the sugars into alcohol are not all resistant to low winter temperatures, fermentation generally went in fits and starts, continuing for up to three months. This produced excessive residual sugar, a certain amount of oxidation and some heavy tannins that only very long aging in wood could mitigate. In other words, a good ten to twelve years would go by between harvesting the grapes and releasing the wine on the market. And even then it was often perceived as top-heavy and excessively alcoholic.

1 Hugh Johnson, *Wine Companion*, Mitchell Beazley, 1984
2 Monica Larner, *Wine Enthusiast*, October 2009.

When Sandro visited the United States for the first time in the late 1960s, he realized that the wine market was evolving and full of opportunity. Consumers who had once been devotees of sweetish wines like Lambrusco had moved on to dry reds, especially those of the Valpolicella. In New York alone Sandro counted 273 different Valpolicella labels, though little in the way of Amarone.

By the early 1970s, however, it was Antinori's new Tuscan wines based on Bordeaux blends that were capturing the attention of both wine writers and discerning drinkers in the United States. This was in itself instructive. Clearly, producers in the Veneto needed to follow the example of their Tuscan counterparts. In other words, it was time to stand back and appraise the wines of Verona objectively, relating their characteristics to what consumers were looking for. At this point Sandro realized that he could beat commercial brands such as Bolla, Folonari and Bertani by producing a new, more balanced and drinkable style of Amarone.

The Masi pursuit of what he later described as "a modern wine with an ancient heart" involved preserving the historical veracity of Amarone, while at the same time improving the balance between fruit and structure, between the requisite acidity and the hint of sweet ripe cherry that lingers in the mouth. During the 1970s, this meant shorter pruning in the vineyard, particular care with the traditional *pergola* training system, its gradual replacement with the trellised Guyot system, and a slight increase in the percentage of the Corvina grape variety in the blend to provide greater depth and structure.

The winery also instigated more rigorous selection of the grapes suitable for appassimento, with a preference for loose bunches which allowed air to circulate around the individual grapes so that they dried out evenly and were unlikely to harbor undesirable molds. This in its turn led to shortening the period in which the bunches of grapes lay on cane trays in the *fruttaio*, or loft, to dry out. With such simple stratagems, Masi was largely able to pre-empt bacterial damage and excessive sugar concentration.

Certain local grape varieties such as Oseleta, Dindarella and Rossignola had been abandoned by most growers since the post-phylloxera reconstruction because their yield in terms of grape juice was low. Guido Boscaini, on the other hand, had tended to preserve them, out of a mixture of respect for past tradition and an appreciation of what we would now call bio-diversity. His intuitive grasp was right in several respects, not least because low juice yields imply a higher skin to flesh ratio, which means more of the anthocyanins present in the skins to give flavor and depth of color to the wine.

Breaking new ground requires constant query, analysis and comparison. At Masi, this takes place in different venues: in the winery's experimental vineyard, where the rare local varietals are rescued from oblivion and put to the test; in the laboratory at the Valgatara winery; down below in the vaulted, underground tasting room that was once the cellar; and in the experimental vineyard at Gargagnago. All these aspects are directed by what is known as the Masi Technical Group, which was formed in 1979. The team consists of experts in enology, viticulture and marketing, and includes Andrea Dal Cin, the winery's enologist; Vittorio Zandonà, a chemist and an enologist by training, who is in charge of quality control; Luc Desroches, the commercial director; Lucio Brancadoro, who oversees the vineyards; and the microbiologist Lanfranco Paronetto, the technical coordinator and Italy's foremost expert in yeasts. Further input comes from several other members with specific roles regarding the technical and economic relationship between the winery itself and various independent growers whose grapes contribute to make the Masi wines.

This Masi Technical Group is the thinking winery's alternative to the hallowed pronouncements of the fashionable itinerant wine-maker. All members have their say and contribute to decision making, which reflects an unusually wide range of concerns. It is directed by Sandro's son Raffaele, a tall, soft-spoken young man more inclined to observe than make statements. While Sandro regularly attends the in-depth tasting sessions that line up not only the Masi wines but also those of other noteworthy producers, it is his son who plans and directs the extent of its activities.

From its inception, the team has worked closely with the Conegliano Institute of Viticulture on vine clone selection, on rootstock for grafting and on the most suitable vine training systems. Since 1985, the Department of Agriculture at Milan University has also been involved, supervising among other things the planting of the substantial experimental vineyard within the Serego Alighieri estate at Gargagnago. The outstanding rediscovery so far has been Oseleta, which now features in the Masi varietal Osar, and blended with Corvina in Toar. It also makes a discreet contribution to the most recent great Masi Amarone, the Riserva di Costasera.

The 1970s also brought to fruition two other major achievements, one of them commercial and the other technical: the launch of the Masi wines in the United States, and the development of a cultivated yeast that could ensure a more even and complete fermentation of semi-dried grapes. The former was based on a more modern approach to promotion that Sandro had been thinking about since his first visit to America. The latter relied on Lanfranco Paronetto's expertise in the microbiology of fermentation.

During Sandro Boscaini's various trips abroad he had begun to see to what extent terroir could play a role in people's perceptions of wine. A region like Tuscany, for instance, already projected an image that producers were able to use to promote their wines. It was as though the perceived idyll of a harmonious landscape vouched for the bottles that derived from them. While art had contributed to the creation of an iconic image for the city of Venice, this was not the case for the Veneto in general, and the Valpolicella in particular. So perhaps it was time to reverse the process, and produce wine that could evoke a landscape in the mind of the consumer.

The first Masi campaign in the USA was launched in 1979. It introduced the Royal Family of Veronese Wines, no less: the King, which was Amarone; and the Prince, in the guise of Campofiorin. It was an impressive sovereign lineup that established lasting contacts not only with importers, wine shops and restaurateurs, but also with the agencies working for the states that exercise a monopoly over the sale of alcohol.

Right from the outset of the Masi enterprise, the idea had been to produce select crus of Amarone that spoke for the different microclimates and soils of the vineyards dotted around the growing area. Thus there was already an Amarone Campolongo di Torbe 1956 ready for release in 1966; and a Mazzano Amarone Classico 1964 in 1971. Between the two, there is already a significant reduction in the time span from vintage to release: eleven years for the former; seven for the latter. Reducing the duration of fermentation meant lessening oxidation and preserving greater fruitiness in the wine, thereby achieving better overall balance without losing complexity. Such were the first fruits of improvements and selection in the vineyard. Then, in 1983, collaboration with Lanfranco Paronetto led to the use of selected strains of the *Saccharomyces bayanus* yeast to effect complete fermentation within a yet shorter time frame of around two months. As a result, maturation in the chosen 600 liter Veronese casks could also be cut back by several years without compromising aging potential in the bottle.

Sandro describes presenting the 1983 Amarone at the 1987 edition of Vinitaly in Verona, when all Masi's competitors were showcasing their newly released 1977s or 1978s. "People shook their heads and said that we had all gone out of our minds," he recalls. "Then they tasted what we were producing and realized that it was something completely different." This was the winery's first example of an Amarone deliberately made to reflect the demands and evolving tastes of an international market.

There was another Masi policy that also caused a stir in Veronese viticulture: the winery's vintage classification and its refusal to make an Amarone in years when the harvest was not good. Sandro describes one telling episode with an ironic smile: "With the 1972 vintage, we knew it wasn't going to make a good enough wine. When word got round that we wouldn't be bottling an Amarone for that year I received numerous phone calls of complaint from winemakers saying, 'Hey, what are you up to? We've already bottled ours . . . .' Another bad vintage was 1982, but by that time people had got used to our independence of spirit."

In 1986 a scandal broke out in the world of Italian wine-making that scared consumers, but ultimately proved a boon for quality viticulture. A number of producers of bulk wines for blending that catered to the bottom end of the market thought they could get away with adding methanol to their products to raise the alcohol content. This adulteration was extremely toxic, causing drinkers to suffer from a range of complaints, from irreversible blindness to liver damage. A few people even died. Understandably, for a while consumers were reluctant to buy wine of any sort. "They were hard times for us too," Sandro admits, "but not for long because we could show our customers exactly where our wines come from. We have direct control over all the vineyards, those of our growers as well as our own. I believe that in the end the shameful methanol experience really made wine lovers realize that there must be a direct relationship between viticulture and winemaking. That may sound obvious, but in years when a number of influential wineries saw fit to blend and bottle products made in other parts of the country, this realization really cleared the deck for quality winemaking."

During the following decade Masi made up for time lost by forging ahead with improvements. Some of these were natural in origin. Climate change brought hotter summers and drier autumns, which resulted in earlier ripening and consequently less risk to the health of the grapes in the drying lofts. Years 1990, 1995 and 1997 were all outstanding vintages that merited the top 5 star rating. But science also had a part to play in the ongoing evolution of the new Masi wines. The introduction of N.A.S.A. (Natural Assisted System for Appassimento), an advanced system for controlling conditions in the drying lofts, meant that humidity could be kept in check and the appassimento process perfected.

By the end of the 1990s, the Masi side of the family enterprise was bursting out of the available space at the Gargagnago villa, which in the meantime had also been adapted to provide offices. As a solution, Sandro, who was still involved in the Boscaini winery, decided to transfer the bottling process to the more spacious Valgatara facility. This resolved part of the problem, at least for a few years. But by 2002 Masi was also short of vineyards. The time seemed ripe for a more radical step. It was decided that the Boscaini winery, which supplied largely to the Italian market, should be put out to pasture. "Various family members were involved in the original business, but it had lacked verve for several years," Sandro explains. "So I drew up a business plan to show them that what we would lose by closing down Boscaini we would make up in a couple of years with Masi, if we were able to take over the other vineyards and all the rest of the Valgatara space."

The entire family rallied around this proposal, though things did not quite evolve as Sandro had predicted. In 2002 the wine market felt the shock waves from the 9/11 tragedy, and it took Masi three rather than two years to catch up with the combined turnover. Since then it has forged ahead, enjoying a substantial return in both image and revenue.

Eight years down the line, however, Sandro is already toying with the idea of returning to Boscaini, the family name, to distinguish a limited production of no more than three or four wines of particular excellence. "Perhaps an Amarone cru, or a varietal," he says, "but not just yet. When the time is right."

II

SHAPING THE LANDSCAPE

Winemakers today like to explain how their wines are an expression of the land, soils and microclimate typical of where they are grown. Such is the all-important concept of *terroir*, which has now made its way into everyday oenophile parlance.

Despite the wide range of winegrowing areas, however, the words used to describe a given terroir generally sound rather similar. To come across as distinctive seems to call for a landscape that has become emblematic, that has connotations beyond viticulture, suggesting a way of life. In this, certain wine-producing regions start off with what appears to be an advantage. If art, film or social history have long highlighted a particular geographical zone, the chances are that people further afield will have an idea in their mind of what the countryside looks like even if they have never been there.

Sandro Boscaini refers to this as "creating a brand linked to the vineyard." It encapsulates the benefits of a well-promoted image. A case in point is Tuscany, which has one of the most iconic landscapes in the world. An unpaved country road flanked by cypress trees winding up a vine-clad hillside, with a silvery olive grove to one side and a well-proportioned stone farmhouse to the other, speaks for Tuscany even to consumers who have yet to set foot in Europe.

Iconic landscapes have their drawbacks, however. Once a visual image becomes an icon, it takes on a degree of immutability that belies reality. The agricultural universe is one of constant change: crops, seasons, weather and farming techniques are all subject to infinite variation. So perhaps the focus should move from emblem to complexity. If wines are able to express such natural complexity, they can be uniquely eloquent. This is certainly true for Amarone. It is an intrinsically complex wine that has much to narrate in terms of landscape.

The Valpolicella Classico growing area is a relatively small district with an astoundingly rich and stratified history. It is not a single valley, as the name might initially suggest, but rather a cluster of three main valleys, and a further six minor ones, each with its own specific soils and climatic peculiarities. Still largely unknown to the wine-drinking public, the 190 square miles of the Valpolicella comprise a mixture of dramatic natural features and simple but ingenious man-made introductions and adaptations implemented over many generations to make the best of what the land has to offer.

Despite the vicinity of the main highway connecting Venice and Milan, most of the Valpolicella preserves a certain magic that is gone from much of the Veneto, where landscape has often been sacrificed at the altar of industry. It is not an area that lends itself to mechanized agriculture. The sloping hillsides have been terraced over the course of time, to prevent seasonal rains from washing away the thin topsoil and to provide the vine roots with moisture released during the summer months by the rocky substratum. Moreover, handsome dry stone walls, known as *marogne,* support the terraces and define property, while deep gullies, many of them wooded, separate one hillside from the next.

Yet the Valpolicella also harbors an industrial vocation, one that has flourished for hundreds of years. This revolves around the quarrying of the mottled pink stone that goes by the toponym *pietra di Prun* and Rosso di Verona marble. The earliest signs of stoneworking in the upper part of the valley date back half a million years. By the Iron Age there were entire villages constructed in stone higher up in the Lessini Mountains. And with the advent of the Ancient Romans, the material was chosen for its warm colors and strength to face buildings and pave roads in Verona and beyond, as the Cavarena district clearly reveals.

Although the worlds of stone and wine may seem antithetical, they intersect in various ways in the Valpolicella. The place name itself seems to suggest a curious overlap. The Ancient Romans referred to the three valleys overlooking Lake Garda as the *pagus Arusnatium*, the Arusnati being the particular ethnic group that populated the area. By the twelfth century, however, the toponym Val Polesela had emerged, in time becoming Valpolicella. Though the etymology of the name has divided historians, most now tend to agree that it derives from the Greek *poly* (many) and the Latin *cella* (cellar, storehouse). In various parts of Italy, from Modica in Sicily to Matera in Basilicata or Pitigliano in Tuscany, caves that resulted from the extraction of stone were used in early modern times for wine storage, so it seems reasonable to imagine that this may also have been the case in the Valpolicella.

Italians use the term *scheletro* meaning "skeleton," to refer to the stony subsoil essential to good viticulture. It suggests the necessary interaction of the earth's hard and soft elements. Certainly the warm, tawny pink of the local stone is as much a feature of the landscape as the bright green of vineyards. Both are accentuated by the almost tactile quality of the light, which softens contours and brings out depth of color. The picture is enriched by two elements that add movement: cherry trees in a flurry of spring blossom, and the perennial silvery shimmer of the olive trees that testify to the mild climate.

Sandro Boscaini describes his experience of this landscape, its inhabitants and culture as the tesserae of a familiar mosaic that has always felt like a comfortable microcosm of peculiarity. "I love the Valpolicella because it's original in so many ways," he declares. "I even love its small contradictions, which seem to suggest a general character that's both sweet and strong, rather like the wines themselves. What's lovable about the valley, its inhabitants and the wine is the fact that they have maintained their identity. The area acts as an interface between the Mediterranean and the Alps, absorbing the best of both worlds."

The elements

Few landscapes are as strikingly elemental as the Valpolicella. Air, fire, earth and water have all played a prodigious role in its formation. What we see today in the hillsides arising to the northeast of the River Adige is a tangible expression of ancient history: as eloquent as Verona's famous monuments, though much older and more subject to gradual change.

Sixty million years ago the area was covered by the vast Tethys Ocean, which extended from the Sahara to the Arctic Circle and Siberia. During the Secondary and Tertiary epochs, known respectively as the Mesozoic and Cainozoic periods, loose material settled on the ocean bed, forming layers of rock sediment that are usually referred to as Jurassic, Cretaceous, Eocene and Miocene.

Between the forming of the Cretaceous and Eocene layers, various underwater volcanoes spread lava over much of the ocean bed, thereby separating one layer of rocky sediment from the next. That was about forty million years ago. Today in various locations throughout the Valpolicella, there are visible strata of basalt, the dark, greenish brown igneous rock known locally as *toari*, and a friable, ochre-colored stone also of volcanic origin. From the mountain pastureland of Sant'Anna d'Alfaedo down to the winegrowing slopes of Mazzano and Torbe and, further south, to the Arbizzano plain, they bear witness to the prodigy of evolution.

What brought the volcanic stone from the bottom of the sea to select areas of the hillside is a story of such magnitude as to challenge the imagination. Towards the end of the Tertiary era, immense forces from the center of the earth started to push the ocean floor upwards until it rose above sea level with a general northeast-southwest inclination. Huge contrasting forces running west to east as far as what is now the Fumane Valley created a fault, which folded the western part of the stratified basin floor, pushing and raising it to an almost vertical position. This movement created the craggy chain that acts as the backbone of the Valpolicella, where the grandiose cone of the Corno d'Aquilio towers above the surrounding pastureland at an altitude of 3,264 feet.

The transformation was completed during the Quarternary Age, one million years ago, when a succession of glacier floods gradually filled the most southerly depressions, forming the terraced plain to the left of the River Adige, from Volargne to Savàl.

When the glaciers began to melt due to a rise in temperatures around 60,000 years ago, abundant water flowed down the three main valleys of Negrar, Marano and Fumane and numerous lesser streams towards the River Adige. The most spectacular of these watercourses is to be found in the upper Fumane Valley, in an area now known as the Molina waterfalls. Flanked on either side by steeply wooded banks, the water tumbles downwards over limestone mounds and outcrops, creating a series of cascades that fill the air with shimmering light and sound.

Once subterranean fire and forces had shaped the Valpolicella, around 600,000 years ago, Neanderthal man was able to hunt on the mountain slopes. It was his modern counterpart who later tracked deer, bison, hare, goat and moose and defended himself from predators such as wolves, fox, bear, hyena and lions. All these creatures, both bi- and quadruped, were drawn by the favorable conditions of the climate and environment.

"Man's skill in taming certain aspects of the landscape without harming it was still evident in my childhood," says Sandro Boscaini. "I have distinct early memories of the Fumane watercourses that were harnessed to turn the wheels for grain and oil mills, and to activate the saws in the timber-yards." Today they are no longer used as a source of power, but the Molina area has at least been well preserved. It has been turned into a park, crisscrossed by footpaths offering some dramatic views and a sense of the boundless raw energy of nature.

The most eloquent emblem of the origins of the Valpo-licella is not a particular site, however. It is an orderly, elegant and ubiquitous coil motif in deep pink to creamy white stone, frequently found in the local quarries. These beautiful patterns were made 150 to 50 million years ago by marine mollusks whose life cycle involved creating a new ring of shell each year. Because the smaller, discarded carapace remained attached to its replacement, in time the series of spirals thus created could reach a diameter of three feet. The magnificent Valpolicella ammonites remind us that history never really repeats itself: rather it reveals themes with infinite variations.

Stone

In 1991 a group of tourists on an excursion to the Similaun glacier, on the Alpine border between Italy and Austria, came across the body of a man buried in the ice. The discovery caused a major international stir because Ötzi, as the mummy was soon called, had lain in his frozen bed for at least five thou-sand years and was, as it were, remarkably well preserved for his age.

Scientists deemed him to be around forty-six years old, and therefore of venerable seniority for someone born between 3,300 and 3,100 B.C.E., when the average life span was around thirty-three. Ötzi's demise was not due to senile frailty, however. He was the victim of a lethal arrow wound, probably inflicted by someone bent on stealing the valuable merchandise he was carrying. This consisted of premium quality arrowheads and other tradable implements made from glassy gray flint. Frag-ments of these wares found on Ötzi's person have revealed them to be from the Valpolicella. In particular, they have been traced to what is probably the greatest natural monument of the area, the Ponte di Veja in the upper Negrar Valley.

The district around the Ponte di Veja had been recognized by toolmakers as an excellent source of raw material for a good 95,000 years before Ötzi started obtaining supplies there. Despite its name[1], the massive arched rock formation that spans a 162-foot gulley was never actually designed as a bridge. It started out as an enormous cave of calcareous rock whose roof fell in, leaving one fifth of the original mass to arch over a ravine at the base of a high cliff, supported by what now appear to be huge sedimentary rock "pillars."

Around the bridge, gigantic chunks of collapsed stone still lie like vanquished Titans on the ground, creating a landscape of dreamlike magnificence. In modern times, excavations near the Ponte di Veja have disclosed numerous vitreous flint tools from the mid- and late-Paleolithic eras. Fifteen such sites dating back over 100,000 years have come to light in the Valpolicella, evidence of Neanderthal Man's industrious presence there. The settlements of the Neolithic period are more numerous, their inhabitants progressing from merely chipping stone implements to polishing them. Such tools would have included knives, awls, scrapers, spear tips and arrowheads: the basic equipment for hunting, making rudimentary attire and fending off assault.

When the discovery of copper provided the hill dwellers with improved implements, they were able to extract stone along the crest of Prun and Monte Loffa. The technique they developed continued unchanged for the next three thousand years, allowing them to erect grouped stone dwellings and villages along high ridges and other relatively safe locations.

What facilitated the labors of quarrymen equipped with Iron Age tools was the fact that the Pietra di Prun consists of around seventy individually named layers of stone ranging in thicknesses from $1\frac{1}{2}$ to $11\frac{1}{2}$ inches. Since each one is neatly separated from the next by a fine layer of clay, it is possible to detach the individual slabs with relatively primitive implements. The curiously rough but even surfaces visible on the stone slabs used for construction and fencing in the uplands are gifts of nature rather than the product of artisanal skill.

---

1 *Ponte* in Italian means "bridge."

The earliest stone settlements have largely been destroyed in the course of time, though significant remains have come to light in the highland area. Foremost among them is the Castellier delle Guàita, built on top of the hill next to the saddle-shaped crest that joins the Fumane and Pantena Valleys. Most of the village is still covered by a thick mantle of pastureland, awaiting future excavation. There is one element that emerges clearly from the ground, however: a counterscarp dating back some 4,000 years, built out of fragments of Cretaceous stone slabs. This wall is probably the oldest man-made rampart in Europe. Yet for all its great age, it speaks for a tangible form of continuity with the present. The basic construction technique can still be found in the *marogne*, or dry stone walls, that are a feature of the present-day Amarone vineyards.

Over the millennia, the extraction of stone has not only supplied tools, provided shelter and defense, and contributed to the construction and embellishment of buildings both within and beyond the Valpolicella. It has also produced unintentional monuments that rival the spontaneous creations of nature and man's deliberate designs.

The most remarkable of these are underground quarries consisting of major vaults and extensive corridors supported by tapering shafts of stone. A document dating back to 1204 reveals that the hillsides near Prun and Torbe have been hollowed out to extract stone for over one thousand years. The technique involved cutting out the naturally formed slabs and leaving lateral columns that widen at the top to support the roof. To the contemporary eye, far from presenting a void, the seven or so miles of these vast tunnels present spatial arrangements reminiscent of the magnificence of Romanesque and early Gothic cathedrals.

Fortunately for posterity, this remarkable heritage has long attracted visitors, whose accounts of what they saw may have contributed to conservation. The Ponte di Veja, for example, is thought to have been an inspiration for the poet Dante. In 1302, when he was banished from his native Florence, he took refuge at the court of Bartolomeo della Scala, seigneur of Verona, and during those years probably spent time in the Valpolicella. There is a passage in the *Inferno* that certainly brings the stone bridge to mind, especially Canto XVIII with its description of the "place in Hell called Malebolge, all of stone, and of an iron color."[2]

In the late nineteenth century, interest in the material culture of the early inhabitants of the Valpolicella spurred archeologists to seek out and save examples of their handiworks. However, these scholars and collectors were not always able to devote time to climbing up the hillsides on foot or horseback to seek out the objects themselves. Instead they generally relied on amateurs among men of some learning, such as the local priest, doctor or pharmacist. This was sometimes a mixed blessing, for in their turn, these gentlemen counted on the good offices of laborers armed with the necessary picks and shovels. To everyone's initial satisfaction, a great number of flints did indeed come to light: the collectors were happy, the local practitioners were gratified, and the laborers received a small reward for their efforts.

Many of these finds were proudly exhibited at the Third International Geography Congress held in Venice in 1881. They provoked widespread debate on account of the occurrence of shapes and motifs hitherto unknown among primitive artifacts. In the 1930s it was discovered that these long-prized items did indeed speak for the creative flair of the local population: not that of its early inhabitants, however, but of the seasonal excavators working on the digs, anxious to supplement their modest economy with a little extra income.

Today, though funding is inevitably short, archeological digs, surveys and analyses are considerably more rigorous. The result is a series of delightfully instructive small museums devoted to the ethnography, the geo-paleontology and the prehistory of the area.

---

2 Dante, *Inferno*, XVIII

Edicts and privileges

Sandro Boscaini describes the identity of the Valpolicella as *appartata*, an adjective that means both "withdrawn" and "isolated," but can also suggest "distinctive." The expression is apt, and not only because the area has always been slightly off the beaten track. The Valpolicella conveys a sense of cohesion that sets it apart. This is not so much to do with geology and landscape, though these elements play their part. It derives from the fact that the area already constituted an organized community well before the Romans arrived towards the end of the third century B.C.E. Moreover, as a geographical and administrative entity, it managed to maintain an unusual degree of autonomy for the following 2,000 years.

Scholars believe that the Arusnati, or inhabitants of the Valpolicella, were of Rhaetian origin, meaning that they descended from the Alpine tribes that populated parts of modern-day Switzerland, Southern Bavaria, most of Tirol and parts of Lombardy in Italy. Language, viticulture and certain objects, both domestic and votive, seem to resemble those of the Etruscans, suggesting extended commercial contacts between the two peoples.

By the early third century B.C.E., the farming community that made up the Pagus Arusnatium was sufficiently evolved to have an administrative center at Fumane, and its religious headquarters on the neighboring hill now occupied by San Giorgio. There were also temples in prominent positions: one in a spectacular setting above Marano, where the church of S. Maria Minerbe now stands, and another at Mazzano, on the site occupied by the parish church. The Arusnati pantheon comprised a Bacchus-like god known as Jupiter Felvenne and other indigenous deities such as Cuslano, who was probably a sun god; Attis, the god of perennial vegetation; and Udisna, the goddess of water.

When Roman expansion began to impinge on the Valpolicella, its inhabitants were permitted a marked degree of administrative autonomy. The imperial rulers adopted a relatively soft approach to their new subjects, nominating a *Pontifex sacrorum Raeticorum*, or High Priest for Rhaetian Rites. Even the word "Pontifex" itself is telling: it is a Latin term that probably derives from the Etruscan, reshaped by folk etymology as if to mean "bridge-maker."

From the year 49 C.E., the area was linked up with other parts of the Empire by means of the Via Claudia Augusta Padana, the road running from Modena towards Germany that wound its way north from Verona beside the River Adige, not far from the present-day SS12. No doubt this artery aided the Rome-ward flow of the Valpolicella's premium product, wine. To judge by a passage in the *Georgics*, it was already a sought-after commodity in the poet Virgil's day, some eighty years earlier: "How shall I praise thee, O Rhaetian grape?" Indeed, recent excavations at Ambrosan, in the centre of the Valpolicella, have brought to light Roman artifacts that prove how those wines relied on the appassimento technique involving semi-dried grapes that is still characteristic of today's Recioto, the semi-sweet wine typical of the area, and its illustrious sibling Amarone.

Five hundred years later, Theodoric the Great, King of the Ostrogoths, invaded Italy and took Verona in 489, making his headquarters in Ravenna and embracing a policy of respect for previously established laws and communities. Like his Roman predecessors, Theodoric particularly enjoyed the wines grown on the hillsides northwest of Verona. In fact his learned prime minister, Cassiodorus, drew up a detailed description of how and where the best wines were made, to ensure supplies to the royal table.

By the dawn of the first millennium, the hillsides of Verona were largely governed by independent communes connected to the parishes of San Giorgio, San Floriano, Arbizzano and Negrar. With the exception of San Floriano, these administrative entities could all count on a castle for defense purposes that included storage space for grain and wine. While some of the properties within these communes were feudal, others belonged to free farmers who still paid certain dues to the local overlord.

The area thus reveals an unusual degree of administrative and fiscal cogency, which in its turn implies an established sense of identity. The name Valpolicella appeared officially for the first time in 1177, but it was probably in common use well before that. At all events, towards the end of the thirteenth century the city of Verona had divided the territory under its jurisdiction into seven *colonnelli*, or outlying districts, the first of which was the Valpolicella. In 1311 this was made over as a feudal possession to Federico della Scala, a member of Verona's ruling dynasty.

Within two years of becoming their overlord, Federico appointed representatives of the Communes and schools to work with specially nominated city authorities in a commission entrusted with the task of establishing the exact confines of the area and its municipal subdivisions. He then proceeded to draw up a notarized agreement defining the expectations and obligations of the city of Verona towards what had become the free County of the Valpolicella, and vice versa. This consisted of nine chapters dealing with mutual defense, repression of crime and free trade, especially regarding wine. Indeed, one late April afternoon in 1320 Federico is said to have headed a procession up to the tiny church at S. Maria in Valverde, overlooking a sea of terraced vineyards, where he solemnly appointed the first *Cavalieri del Recioto*, or Knights of Recioto, who still have a somewhat theatrical following today. Clearly the arrangement between Verona and the Valpolicella was more a treaty between two states intent on harmonious collaboration than a declaration of vassalage.

Just over a decade later, however, Federico fell out of favor with his uncle Cangrande della Scala, the powerful seigneur of Verona much admired by Dante, and was duly banished. By 1387, however, the della Scala family was ousted from power, and the peaceable inhabitants of the Valpolicella found themselves caught up in a series of armed struggles between Venice and Padua. Verona capitulated in 1405, judging that allegiance with Venice was more likely to bring peace and prosperity; and the Valpolicella lost no time in following suit.

The Most Serene Republic of Venice had accumulated power and riches over the previous centuries through trade with the east, from Constantinople to Damascus, Persia, India and beyond. Among other things, the city-state acquired hemp for making the ropes for sailing ships, which contributed to its maritime superiority. It also carried spices from the east to markets in the west, loading up with select western goods on the return journey. Moreover, it held a total monopoly of salt, which was an essential household commodity.

The wealth thus accrued funded the construction and embellishment of fine palaces and churches, but Venice itself and the outlying islands offered limited building space for exhibiting such splendor. So, early in the 1400s, Doge Francesco Foscari decided on mainland expansion. This involved co-opting cities and estates, starting with Vicenza, Feltre and Belluno in 1404 and continuing, as we have seen, with Verona, followed by Padua, in 1405. Over the next fifteen years, much of the rest of the Veneto, along with the cities of Friuli and the Trentino, also expressed their *dedizione*, or submission to Venice.

In general, these new territories realized that Venice would exercise sovereignty with foresight, aware of the mutual benefits to derive from flourishing dominions. Right from the outset, however, the Valpolicella enjoyed particular privileges, no doubt partly due to its potential strategic importance in the defense of the northern borders. A *Rettore*, elected in Venice from among the local aristocracy, was sent as a governor to each of the newly annexed cities to oversee the administration of justice. In the case of the Valpolicella, however, it was agreed that a magistrate from Verona should be elected each year by the Valley Council to act as *Vicario*, or representative of the Doge. His tasks involved dealing with administrative, fiscal and judicial matters in keeping with an edict entitled "The Privileges and Rights of the Valpolicella."[3]

The Villa and the Farmhouse

The prosperity that came with a period of prolonged peace under Venetian domination made a tangible impact on both the cities and the countryside. To the Venetian nobility, maritime trade no longer seemed the safest way to accumulate wealth, whereas investing in property on the mainland was more reassuring, and indeed enjoyable. Verona was soon embellished with handsome new *palazzi*, churches and public squares, while the Valpolicella saw the construction of magnificent villas surrounded by carefully planned gardens designed to mediate between the private world of the grand manor house and the farmland beyond.

This was not an entirely new trend. For centuries Veronese landowners had deemed it opportune to have major dwellings in the Valpolicella, so that they could pay the occasional extended visit to their rural possessions to keep an eye on farm revenues. It was less common for the owners to reside permanently in their country properties.

A notable exception to this general rule is the Serego Alighieri family at Gargagnago. It was Dante's son Pietro, a judge in Verona, who in 1353 acquired the initial property consisting of a house and land. Referred to in the deeds as the Casal dei Ronchi estate, the original nucleus comprised vineyards, which were increased in extension through further purchases over several generations. Clearly this part of the Valpolicella was already recognized as an excellent growing area, producing grapes that commanded premium prices and supplying the Verona cellars with an impressive amount of wine.

The family's decision to reside in the country property was probably a virtue of necessity. The land, which would have been rented to tenant farmers or sharecroppers, was in all likelihood

---

3 This was published in book form by the humanist abbot G.G. Pigari in 1588.

burdened with tithes and perpetual leases that had to be paid to the churches and monasteries that were the original owners. Not only were there deadlines to meet for payments due; there were schedules to respect for collecting rents, renewing contracts, inventorying produce that flowed into the estate and providing storage for it. To make such an investment viable meant overseeing and directing the whole complex system firsthand, which is what probably encouraged the original Alighieri family to make this their home. At the outset, the dwelling was more of a grand farmhouse than a villa, and probably remained so until some time after 1549, when Marcantonio Serego married Ginevra Alighieri, linking his name to hers so that the great poet's family did not become extinct for lack of a male heir.

Additions were made to the house at Gargagnago over the following century, gradually turning it into the villa we see today, where the poet's descendants still reside. The property includes separate farm buildings on a grand scale, surrounding an ample quadrangular courtyard. It is this latter section of the property, along with the vineyards, that is now managed in collaboration with Masi. Two sides of the farm buildings house the winemaking facilities, including the cellars and the traditional airy lofts for drying out the grapes; the other two have been turned into guests' accommodation and reception rooms.

A number of fortified farmhouses in the Valpolicella were gradually turned into villas in the late fifteenth century, though many of the most famous were new constructions, built at the behest of patrician landowners. What changed with the sixteenth century, no doubt as a result of Venetian influence, was the unprecedented degree of comfort and elegance of these magnificent residences. Thus planned, equipped and decorated, they could accommodate a microcosm of patrician society in its transfer from city to rural arcadia.

An early example of the new cult of the sumptuous manor house was Villa della Torre at Fumane. It was built in the mid-sixteenth century at the behest of Girolamo della Torre, a humanist scholar engaged in significant social, political and religious activities. The owner himself may well have had a hand in the designs, working closely with the architect and painter Giulio Romano, Raphael's pupil whose opus includes Villa Lante in Rome and Palazzo Te in Mantua. Villa della Torre now belongs to the Allegrini winery, producers of some fine Amarone and Valpolicella Classico that have met with widespread national and international praise.

By the late sixteenth century, a grand residence in the country had become more than a convenience for landowners anxious to keep an eye on the management of their property, especially in areas such as the Valpolicella, where the climate was mild and inviting. By expanding in size and comfort, the villas of the Veneto were becoming an enchanted occasional refuge for the urban nobility and leisured classes, who had rediscovered the delights of nature-at least of nature duly tamed in the shape of an extensive and varied garden overlooking the farmland.

Half a generation later, one of the most influential architects of the entire sixteenth century was also busy with designs for villas in the Valpolicella. This was Andrea Palladio, who had been commissioned by Marcantonio Serego to transform the large Santa Sofia manor house near Pedemonte into a villa befitting so prominent a family. Serego himself was not only a man of means; he also had vision, contributing enormously to the development of Veronese agriculture in his time. Palladio was duly impressed by patron, location and surroundings. He praised the extensive gardens and graceful fountains, and set out to design a dwelling of great classical elegance, but on a massive scale.

As often happens, the whole project went well beyond budget, and was halted when less than a quarter had been accomplished. For the noble patron, this over-extension was unlikely to have been ruinous, since he had already married Ginevra Alighieri and taken up residence at Gargagnago. Yet the mixture of farsightedness and overreaching ambition that underlies the collapse of many a grand worldly project seems to have haunted Santa Sofia like a pale ghost. For it was here, over four hundred years later, that poor commercial management brought about the collapse of what had been a promising winery, leaving the enologist Nino Franceschetti free to take up the new Masi venture proposed to him by the Boscaini family.

Another winemaking family has taken over the Santa Sofia estate and is establishing a name for itself, aided by the added value of the historic premises. Like the Masi collaboration with Serego Alighieri, these are both examples of the growing awareness of the benefits of image. It's essential to have well-located and tended vineyards, but if these revolve around a beautiful historic villa, where the walls themselves have absorbed a sense of elegance and taste, there is much to be gained in terms of context and connotation.

One of the first wineries to perceive the added value of a magnificent setting was Bertani, whose Soave white wine graced the royal menu for the coronation feast of King George VI in 1937. Though the original Bertani estate was in the Valpantena, which is due east of the Valpolicella, in the early 1950s the family acquired Villa Fattori-Mosconi at Novare, a magnificent country residence surrounded by sixty acres of parkland facing south, towards the Arbizzano plain. The interiors, richly frescoed and decorated with ornate plasterwork and *trompe l'oeil* niches, are remarkable. But equally noteworthy are the cellars, which were already deemed "ample, convenient, noble and famous" in the eighteenth century, when successive owners invested in improvements. Wine was becoming a serious business. When Luigi Trezza, a wealthy Veronese expert in viticulture, bought the estate in 1868, only seventy-four of its 568 acres were planted with vines. Within the space of eight years he had increased that to 210 acres, adding a further 198 in the 1890s.

Given the history of the Valpolicella, it is not surprising that the concept of agriculture as an enterprise took root there relatively early. Clearly the idea of growing wines for distant markets was a radical deviation from the age-old arrangement whereby tenant farmers and sharecroppers tilled the soil to provide food for their own tables, and income in the form of rent or produce for the landowner. The increase in the areas devoted to viticulture that accompanied a focus on export changed the landscape considerably. Preparing ground for vines meant removing rocks and stones to below the depth of a ploughshare; in those days it also involved planting fruit trees as vine supports, or constructing a trellis to hold up a pergola.

The grand country houses also modified to some extent the way people related to the landscape, both the rich and the poor. For the villa owners and their guests, the creation of a garden transcended the idea of merely creating a pleasant environment for a stroll. To illustrate this point it is worth taking one of the finest gardens of the Valpolicella as an example. The Giardino di Pojèga was designed in 1783 by the architect Luigi Trezza[4] for Count Antonio Rizzardi, whose descendents still own the villa and produce wine on the property. The Count had inherited a passion for gardening from his forebears, and was determined to create a garden "containing secret places such as those poets and philosophers once contemplated in admiration," with a center that was to be "the heart's desire": a fountain rotunda embraced by an outer ring of cypress, myrtle and laurel. At the Count's behest, the architect set out to reconcile the informality typical of late eighteenth century design with the formal layout of previous centuries, combining perspectives with trees and lawns, in keeping with the then-fashionable English gardens. The outcome is like a series of microcosms ingeniously linked by tree-lined avenues or flights of steps. But the most fascinating outdoor space is what was known as a *teatro di verzure*. This is a "greenery" amphitheater with seven tiers of box clipped to resemble the intersecting flights of stone steps. All around are box and cypress hedges, and niches of hornbeam containing statues representing mythological characters from Greek theater. It was on stages such as this that Venetian culture, expressed in the comedies of Carlo Goldoni and his followers, mirrored the mores and preoccupations of the privileged society that made up the audience. Nature had become an art form, and thus idealized could interact with other manifestations of human creativity.

---

4 Not the same Luigi Trezza who was later to purchase Villa Fattori-Mosconi.

The grand villas of the Valpolicella tended to share a number of features: an extensive garden as an appurtenance of the main house; a wider park enveloping both this residence and the farm buildings that created a U-shape around a courtyard; and the dwellings of sharecrop farmers, some of them among the farm buildings, and others located further away, both within and beyond the *brolo*, or orchard and vegetable gardens enclosed by the dry stone walls that encircled the entire property. When, in the early twentieth century, sharecrop farming came to an end as demands for salaried labor ousted the earlier system, certain characteristics of villa layout found their way into the farmhouses built by smallholders and tenant farmers. The most evident of these was the custom of building on three sides of a courtyard, leaving the fourth side for the entrance. Known as the *corte veneta*, this arrangement often incorporated the dwellings of more than one family, creating an economy of scale that could include the sharing of equipment, and providing solidarity—no doubt occasionally interspersed with feuds—among farming families still largely tied to a subsistence economy.

The houses of both the laborers who lived on the big estates and the independent farmers usually comprised a simple dwelling on the ground floor, and a spacious attic under the roof. Air circulated through these lofts via low windows under the eaves, making them ideal for drying the grapes during the appassimento process. So from harvesting through to February, the *fruttai*, as the lofts are called, were filled with large cane trays stacked one above the other, each bearing select bunches of grapes laid out to dry. While this operation clearly related to the economy of the estate, the farming families were also able to use the lofts from April through to mid-June for raising silkworms. This was usually the job of the womenfolk, including the girls. Supplies of fresh mulberry leaves had to be taken up to the loft every five hours to feed the voracious creatures as they spun their cocoons of silken thread; the cocoons themselves had to be kept clean; and once they had grown to full size, nimble fingers plunged them into boiling water to get them ready for sending to the spinning factories. It was hard work, but did bring in a little extra income. Though such cottage industry implied contacts with the outside world, in its essence it mirrored the inward-looking focus of early twentieth century farm life in the Valpolicella. It was only after the Second World War that ways of life in the countryside, and the houses that contained them, began to reflect the new developments that were gradually having an impact on Italian society.

Change

The agricultural community was thus singularly tight-knit and self-sufficient, busy with interrelated activities that led from one season to the next. It was a hardworking society that tended to be conservative, since change would have implied realignment of its many stratified components. When landowners did see the need for innovation, they would have had to set up a system of pyramidal persuasion: first the farm manager would have to understand the new project, so that the laborers themselves could be told what to do. In the case of viticulture, this often went against the grain. Those landowners who understood that hard pruning and grape selection in the vineyard were essential to improvement in wines found it difficult to get their workers to follow the new instructions. Sandro remembers how hard it was to persuade them. "For those uneducated laborers whose only school had been customary practice, discarding certain bunches of grapes or trying to get the vines to produce less must have been like offending God in his bounty."

The greatest changes came about for external reasons, however. Since the early 1900s, the Valpolicella had been crossed east to west by a railway line linking Verona to Lake Garda. In the 1950s, this was replaced by what is now the valley road that connects up the municipalities of S. Ambrogio, San Pietro in Cariano and Negrar. Automobile transport forged new contacts between the inhabitants of these areas and the city, opening up the possibility of finding work in the nascent valley industry. Farm hands who had hitherto had little choice about how they earned a living suddenly found themselves with a number of different options, including salaried labor in factories. At much the same time, new agricultural machinery was also making its first appearance, promising to do the job of several families' worth of sharecroppers.

"When I was a boy the landscape of the Valpolicella was practically cut off from the rest of the world," recalls Sandro Boscaini. "There were two different types of agriculture—that of the peasant farmers who just about made a living from their efforts, and that of the relatively well-to-do, such as my family, but also the aristocracy. So there were the fine villas, some of them long neglected, the farmhouses and small villages with just one store selling everything from dry goods to meat, including salt and tobacco, which were state monopolies. Then of course there was the cobbler, the barber and the blacksmith. But there were no greengrocers in those days. People made do with what they grew in their *brolo*, or fruit and vegetable garden. Any glut in production was carefully stored or bottled so that it lasted most of the year."

In those days, signs of the outside world only reached the towns that had a railway station. The roads leading to the villages on the hillsides above the valley were unpaved, and life was, as Sandro puts it, "not so much poor as simple." For facilities like a pharmacy, a post office or a cinema, the inhabitants of the Valpolicella had to go down to Pedemonte or San Pietro, in proximity to the railway line—towns that boasted a smattering of Art Nouveau architecture that spoke for links with life beyond the valley. But at Fumane, Valgatara and Marano these things were unheard of. Sandro's primary education took place at the village school. With a hint of envy he describes the lot of children who lived too far away to go home for lunch. "They brought a chunk of bread with them and were free to go off bird-nesting in the early afternoon, whereas we were subject to all the usual parental lunchtime scrutiny," he recalls. "What's more, they wore shoes with hob-nailed wooden soles, which made a fantastic noise on hard ground. I thought that was wonderful. But I was forced to wear proper leather shoes."

From the age of eleven, Sandro was dispatched to a board-
ing school in Verona, from which he only returned for the
holidays. During the long summer months at home, however,
he enjoyed a luxury denied to most of the farm lads of his age:
mobility, in the shape of a bicycle, a passion he has maintained
to this day. He used to meet up with cousins and friends in the
village square, alternating boyish exploits in the local woods and
streams with trips down to the "modern" railway towns. Then
there was the two-week stay at the seaside down on the Adriatic coast, and the period spent up in the mountains above the
Valpolicella, where the air was pleasantly cool at the height of
summer, and the accent and dialect of the local children almost
foreign. Perhaps this early awareness of the existence of different worlds encouraged the sort of mental elasticity that Sandro
would describe as typical of the Venetian entrepreneur.

During the summer months, the winegrowers of the Valpolicella pay particular attention to the sky, which frequently
unleashes freak storms due to the clash of warm breezes that
rise from the lake and cold winds that blow down the Adige
Valley from the north. On occasions, these cloudbursts are accompanied by hail of a size that smacks more of folk legend
than real measurement, were it not for the fact that even in
recent times the phenomenon has repeated itself: in 2002, for
instance, when hailstones weighing 600 grams, the size of a
peach, were reported and photographed.

In storms such as these winemakers can watch as the work
and investment of a whole year is torn to shreds. "We produced
no Amarone in 2002 because the quality of the remaining grapes
simply wasn't good enough," Sandro recalls. "You can't raisin
grapes unless they're in perfect condition; otherwise they'll be
attacked by harmful molds. When I was a child people often
created amulets in the hope of protecting themselves from hail.
My grandfather, for example, used to hang little crosses made
out of olive branches blessed at Easter on each row of vines.
The attitude was: 'We can't do anything about it, but surely the
Creator can.' Then in the late 1950s and early 1960s, technology
was roped in for the same cause, though to little effect, other

than noise. Special cannons were installed on the hilltops over-looking the vineyards to shoot any threatening clouds. The heat of the shot was supposed to melt the hail. It wasn't really very effective, but as kids we thought it created an amazing show, with flashing trails mixing with the lightning and the bangs that seemed to compete with the roar of the thunder."

Nature permitting, after the summer came the grape harvest. Following the first selection of bunches suitable for appassimento, the men and women who tended the various Boscaini vineyards would place the harvested grapes in an elongated tub that sat on the cart, harnessed and ready to be taken down to the winery. Before it left, men with bare feet would tread the bunches down, to make room for more. At the cellars, the grape juice and skins were transferred to the presses by the bucketful. Sandro recalls this as being one of the best parts of the operation, because the children were usually supplied with a bottle or two of fresh grape juice to take home, where it would be cooked and reduced into a sort of compote known as *sugolo*.

It is especially fitting, however, that one of the great spectacles of Sandro's childhood should epitomize the sudden convergence of ancient and modern in mid-twentieth century agriculture: the arrival of the combine harvester. Because the Boscainis had a substantial farm property, they used to hire this roaring giant of a machine for a couple of days up at the Valgatara estate. But the fun really began when the lumbering colossus took up residence in the village square so that tenant farmers and smallholders in the surrounding district could bring their wheat sheaves down by ox-drawn cart for processing. It was noisy, dusty and efficient in an excitingly voracious way. What's more, while the grain was separated from the chaff, another part of the machine was busy producing neat oblong bales of straw that provided the children with a job. This involved clipping the two bands of wire that held the bales together, an art that engendered some fierce competition.

Because this enormous piece of equipment did in a few days what numerous families would have taken several weeks to accomplish, the farmers suddenly found themselves in a position to devote more time to other cultivations. Moreover, there were similar developments in the economy of viticulture, with major investment in modern cellars. "At a certain point my father decided it was time to update our equipment," Sandro recalls. "This involved replacing the old wooden fermentation vats with cement ones. These were huge containers that were cast in concrete on the spot and then finished with steel detailing. To our eyes then, they were totally futuristic. All the digging down to create the space for the vertically stacked vats was done by hand, with a pickaxe, but to take away the excavated earth we had a little train of the sort they use in mines. Of course, this was a major attraction for us kids. Each child had his favorite cart, and we used to ride on top of the moving load of soil and stones." Winery renovation also involved the process of crushing the grapes. A reinforced cement vat was installed at ground level to contain the harvested fruit. Beneath this was the *garolla*, an ingenious piece of machinery designed to de-stem and crush the grapes. The juice and skins dropped down into another vat below, and from here could be transferred to cement fermentation vats by means of flexible rubber pipes.

This was the last word in modernity and hygiene. But before long even the cement vats were considered passé, giving way to more practical stainless steel tanks that could even be moved if necessary. Everything is relative, of course: today cement fermentation vats are making an unexpected comeback.

A hitherto unimaginable degree of rationalization was way under. Agriculture was slowly becoming a business, shaped by investment aimed at producing an income that transcended mere subsistence. This paved the way for other forms of mechanization that were to change the face of farming and rural society, impinge upon landscape and forge the future of the Italian mechanical industry.

III

THE GENTLE GIANT

Just as certain people appear larger than life, literally or metaphorically, so there are wines that stand out for their stature. Both can be a little daunting, especially at the outset. This may explain why for many years critics were loath to acknowledge Amarone. "It was as though wine writers were all set up for appraising a Cabernet Sauvignon, a Merlot or a Sangiovese, but simply didn't have the critical parameters for grape varieties that are unique to the Valpolicella, and a wine made with highly individual techniques that date back many centuries," says Sandro Boscaini. "Amarone was clearly an imposing wine, but without the aggressive punch of the usual enological heavyweights. Instead it was rounded, intriguing and persuasive."

If the mountain will not come to Mohammad, Mohammad must go to the mountain. So in 1995 Sandro presented an exclusive tasting of Amarone in the New York offices of *Wine Spectator*, including bottlings of the single cru Mazzano, spanning 1941–1990. As Bruce Sanderson, the magazine's tasting director, was later to report, "It provided an excellent opportunity to understand the confusing nature of this 'gentle giant.'"[1]

The expression is wonderfully apt, conjuring up the surprise of someone who discovers that what is prodigious can also be kindly, inviting, subtle and profound. Yet the description also

---

1 *The Wine Spectator*, 1996

falls short of reality. The prime inhabitant of the Valpolicella is not a single giant, but a whole family of epic beings who speak for particular hillsides and valleys.

People have long been aware of the variety of growing areas in the Valpolicella. The State Archives in Verona conserve a contract drawn up in the year 1194 between the Monastery of San Zeno, feudatory overlords of the entire Negrar valley, and a certain Musio di Panego, who leased land from the fiefdom. In this agreement the rent was stipulated not in monetary terms, but as a quantity of grapes from two vineyards that today produce some of Masi's finest crus: the Mazzano estate, and the upper reaches of the Torbe growing area.

Spread over deeply sloping hillsides high up in the prime growing area, Mazzano enjoyed the benefits of light summer breezes that helped the grapes ripen in perfect condition. What made the Torbe vineyard so special was the presence of volcanic soils rich in basalt from the Eocene age, known in the local dialect as *toari*. These tend to be deep, loose and well-drained, with sufficient natural humus and good chemical and mineral balance. They contribute to the gentle tannins and hints of almond and mineral typical of one of Masi's flagship Amarones, the Campolongo di Torbe.

So the historic document illustrates at least three different points: that within the relatively narrow confines of the Valpolicella there are different soils and microclimates that produce recognizably different wines; that awareness of this fact has long been widespread; and that medieval monks did not stint themselves in their votive libations.

Sandro Boscaini likens the homeland of the giant family to a Futurist painting. The mixed metaphor is a little startling, but eloquent. While it clearly does not embrace the Futurists' declared rejection of the past, it does suggest what those early twentieth century artists described as "dynamic sensation," whereby "all things move, all things run, all things are rapidly changing."[2] In terms of landscape, this means not only

---

2 2nd Manifesto of Futurist Painters, 11 April, 1910.

the transformations in color, light, cultivation and even sound that come with the changing hours and seasons, but also the constant impact of man equipped with tools with which to shape the environment according to his needs. It's a curious coincidence that the artist who most effectively portrayed this fragmentation of reality should be Umberto Boccioni. Although he was not a Venetian by birth, he studied painting in Venice, and died and is buried near Verona.

Within the "moving picture" of the Amarone growing area, however, there are constants essential to the birth and development of the wine. These revolve around two unique phenomena: indigenous grape varieties with distinctive characteristics, and the creation of a dry wine using the appassimento technique. Though both are part and parcel of the overall environment, they are so unusual as to each require its own narration.

Grape Varieties

Verona has always been a natural crossroads for migration. The Adige Valley, which borders the Valpolicella to the west, provided a route towards the north, the flatlands of the Po Valley facilitated access from the west, and navigation of the narrow Adriatic Sea meant that it was also relatively simple to reach the area from the south and east. In early times, when people left their homeland in search of somewhere else to settle, the one thing they could easily take with them was vine cuttings. This explains why Verona, and the Valpolicella in particular, enjoys a singularly rich heritage of grape varieties.

In recent years scholars and scientists have analyzed the germplasm of Veronese vines to try to understand where they originally came from. It is generally agreed, however, that the many species introduced from the east, like others first cultivated in the Mediterranean basin, so readily adapted to their new environment that over the centuries they grew apart from the matrix, with which they would now reveal only minimal shared characteristics.

The mild weather and mineral-rich soils of the area must have contributed to the forging of these new identities. That the vines did particularly well in their new home is testified around 77–79 C.E. by Pliny the Elder. In his *Natural History*, he declares that Virgil was particularly fond of the Veronese raisined wines, describing the vines that produced them as "preferring the temperate climate and having a great love for their land, such that when transplanted elsewhere they leave all their glories and good qualities behind."[3]

Archaeological evidence also bears witness to the primacy of Veronese wines at the outset of the first millennium—a Roman-Arusnatian statuette in terracotta portraying a priestess bearing a wine jug, for instance, and numerous bowls and jugs in chased bronze for serving wine. An inscription on a fragment of bronze found in 1891, and then lost again, also reveals that by the end of the second century C.E. the city had developed a commercial port for the *negotiatores vinorum* at Sant'Anastasia on the River Adige, whence the fine wines were exported to distant markets.

The precious rarity of this vine patrimony has long been the subject of comment. In 503 C.E., some five hundred years after Pliny dwelt on the matter, it featured in a detailed letter written by Cassiodorus, whose job as first minister to the Ostrogoth King Theodoric the Great comprised locating and organizing supplies of the best possible produce for court banquets. "A well-furnished royal table is a credit to the State," the minister declared. "A private person may eat only the produce of his own district, but it is the glory of a King to collect at his table the delicacies of all lands … It becomes a King so to regale himself that he may seem to foreign ambassadors to possess almost everything … We therefore order you to visit the cultivators of Verona, and offer them a sufficient price for this product of theirs … It is in truth a noble wine and one that Italy may be proud of. Inglorious Greece may doctor her wines with foreign admixtures, or disguise them with perfumes. There

---

3 *Natural History*, xiv, 25–26.

is no need of any such process with this liquor. It is purple, as becomes the wine of kings. Sweet and strong, it grows more dense in tasting it, so that you might doubt whether it was a liquid food or an edible drink."[4]

In the course of time, the great wealth of grape varieties dwindled. Farmers naturally tended to abandon those that did not do well in company with other vines, or produced poor or little fruit. Thus by the late eighteenth century winegrowers had largely reduced their plantings to four or five varieties. There were still plenty of others, but a degree of selection had become normal viticultural practice.

This continued up to the late twentieth century, when the classic trio of Corvina, Rondinella and Molinara, in slightly varying percentages, became the accepted norm for the production of both Amarone and its fresh younger sibling, the Valpolicella classico red. Masi, however, continued to nurture interest in some of the neglected varieties, saving many from extinction.

Sandro had often wondered how the Valpolicella red had managed to establish itself on foreign markets alongside more structured and imposing wines, such as those of Bordeaux, Piedmont and Tuscany. In time he had come to believe that small amounts of forgotten grapes grown in hillside vineyards might have given it greater individuality and stature. Moreover, in those days only a small percentage of premium bunches was set aside for drying, which meant that the overall quality of the Valpolicella red was probably remarkably high.

In 2000, these hypotheses culminated in a far-sighted project involving the Masi Technical Group in collaboration with the Department of Viticulture and Enology of the University of Milan, and the Rauscedo Grapevine Nurseries Cooperative in Friuli: the planting of an experimental vineyard on the Serego Alighieri property and the establishment of an experimental winemaking facility in which small batches of drying grapes

---

4 Flavius Magnus Aurelius Senator, Cassiodorus, Letter to the Canonicarius of the Venetiae. Book XII, IV *In Praise of Acinaticium, a red wine of Verona*, 503 A.D.

and wine could be kept under constant surveillance. This facility was equipped to analyze all aspects of the particular clones, the most appropriate rootstocks, the grape varieties rescued from oblivion, behavior during appassimento and vinification, and the influence of aging in different types of cask.

"With Attilio Scienza's expert guidance, to plant the experimental vineyard we became the Sherlock Holmes of grape growing, ready to follow any lead that might bring us to extant examples of ancient varieties so that we could mark them when the foliage and fruit made them still recognizable, and then take winter cuttings for propagation the next spring," Sandro recalls. "Out of the forty-eight varieties and clones we managed to plant, it became clear that the most promising were Dindarella, Croatina, Negrara, Forselina and Oseleta. But it was the Oseleta that rewarded us with the most interesting results. The grapes, which are not prolific, are small with relatively large pips, which means the juice obtained from them during crushing is a good thirty percent less than for other varieties. That's probably why it was abandoned. But the skins are thick and dark, investing the wine with magnificent, deep color and plenty of berry aromas, while the pips, when fully ripe, provide very pleasant tannins. In 1985 we planted two hectares of Oseleta, and in 1990 came out with Toar, a blend of Corvina and Oseleta that marries the value of indigenous grapes with the stature of the finest international wines. We were so happy with this outcome that we decided to produce the Oseleta varietal wine we called Osar. It's unusually complex and well-structured for the Verona area, with extraordinary depth of color and body, and wonderful aging potential. Oseleta also proved to be very promising when semi-dried. The small amount that is added to the Amarone Costasera Riserva, Masi's most recent Amarone, results in a wine with greater tannic structure and exceptional color. You could call it a new type of Amarone, one that stands up to comparison with the great reds of the world, but without losing its originality. Getting to know Oseleta has been like meeting a wise old friend you'd lost sight of, and discovering he has retained all his youthful energy, rounded out with the wisdom of maturity."

Considerable effort has been devoted to understanding exactly what Corvina, Rondinella and Molinara, plus Oseleta, the old-established newcomer, impart to Amarone. Research has centered on the intrinsic characteristics of the grapes themselves, how they interact, how they behave during appassimento, and how the musts thus obtained evolve individually and together during fermentation and aging.

"In the first place there must be rigorous selection in the vineyard," Sandro insists. "It is here that we identify the bunches best suited to drying, harvesting them separately once they are fully ripe. The shape of the bunch is important, because when it's very compact air cannot circulate between the individual grapes, which means that tiny mold pockets could develop on the vine or after picking. Straggly bunches, on the other hand, avoid this problem because the fruit enjoys all round aeration. Of course, the grapes must ripen evenly and be in perfect health to give of their best when dried."

In particularly bad years, when adverse weather conditions compromise the quality of the grapes, Masi simply renounces making any Amarone. This was the case in 1982, 1984, 1987, 1992 and 2002. And only a limited selection will be singled out for drying when prevailing conditions have been average. For an exceptional vintage, on the other hand, between thirty and sixty percent of the harvest will undergo appassimento and be used for Amarone.

The Corvina variety, which accounts for 70–75% of the blend in the Masi Amarones, grows well in all the different soils of the Valpolicella, producing compact, pyramidal bunches of grapes weighing about 150 grams that ripen in late September-early October. When fresh, these grapes provide good structure and slightly herbaceous notes not found in the other members of the classic trio. During appassimento they are subject to *Botrytis*. The Rondinella is obligingly productive, consistent and particularly resistant to blight, which for many years made it particularly popular. It contributes color and tannins, and to-day holds a 25% stake in the Masi Amarones. This is reduced to 15% in the case of the Riserva di Costasera, where Oseleta makes up for it in terms of depth of color and flavor. Molinara, the third variety, has also diminished in importance, probably because it lacks body and color. However, Masi has always appreciated the way its good acidity contributes to the drinkability and spice tones of Amarone, which are important features in wines of great concentration.

Vine training has also undergone considerable change. The time-honored practice of using trees such as ash, elm and willow as "live" supports for vines gradually gave way to more rational systems, particularly the pergola. An early illustration of grape harvesting involving the use of triangular ladders erected around and beside the tree trunk shows how high up those bunches must have grown, and how potentially perilous gathering them must have been. But even the early pergolas were tall enough, to judge by a miniature preserved in Verona's Biblioteca Civica portraying a group of learned humanists talking beneath a pergola twice their height.[5] There is also evidence that since Roman times a third system was common in the flatter areas, where vines were pruned back and tied to poles, *ad jugum allevate*, meaning "trained to the yoke."[6]

By the fifteenth century, in the prime growing areas of the Valpolicella both of the first two systems were common, though the grapes grown on vines that were "enslaved" (*vineis sclavis*), or pruned and tied to supports, fetched a higher price than those harvested from vines "married" to trees that were often grown in rows between strips of arable land. It was only in the second half of the twentieth century that the structures supporting the vines were positioned to provide comfortable access for pruning and harvesting.

---

5 Manuscript 2072, "De Thermis Calderianis," Biblioteca Civica, Verona.
6 Both Martial and Pliny use this expression, which is found again in at least two contracts regarding land use and ownership, dating back to the years 894 and 1063. See *Oseleta, Model for Viticulture in the Venetian Area*, Fondazione Masi, Verona, 2006, p. 42.

"When I was young the pergola was still the norm on the hillside terraces," Sandro confirms. "It's a system that has come in for a lot of unjust criticism because it tends to encourage excessive fruit production, at the expense of intensity of aromas and color. However, with careful management, meaning plenty of hard pruning, it can be very effective because it ensures good exposure to sun and ventilation, as well as keeping the grapes well off the ground so they're not subject to humidity and mold. The pergola also produces wonderfully concentrated grapes at the end of the long branches known as *filagne*, which can be trained to arch over the terrace. This is because the vine has to put extra energy into nurturing its fruits at such a distance from the matrix."

By the beginning of the twenty-first century, the pergola had largely given way to a system not dissimilar to the training *ad jugum alleviate* first experimented by the ancient Romans: trellises (the *juga*) supporting more densely planted vines, cane pruned and trained according to the Guyot system.

Technique

Amarone embodies a curious dichotomy. It is made with a technique that can be traced back over two thousand years, yet it is not an ancient wine. Less than fifty years ago it was not even officially recognized as a wine in its own right, but was considered a "dry" version of Recioto, the opulent sweet wine for which the Valpolicella was renowned.

The explanation for this apparent contradiction involves the history of taste as much as it does the history of appassimento in the Valpolicella. In the days when terracotta amphorae were used to carry wines to the Imperial table in Rome, the only way to keep the precious cargo from going sour before reaching its destination was to make sure it was either very alcoholic or very sweet, perhaps with the addition of honey or resin. In either case, on arrival the wine could be watered down, or adulterated with various substances, as Cassiodorus disdainfully pointed out. An alternative was to transport the grapes themselves to Rome, since there was no point in transplanting the vines, precisely because they did not fare well beyond the Verona hillsides. Here again, it was a question of partially drying the fruit to concentrate the sugars and aromas, then carefully packing it into urns. In the days before sugar was commercially available, sweetness in the form of fructose was both a necessity and a luxury: it was a natural preservative, and a delectable rarity. Bearing this in mind, it is evident the wines enjoyed by the ancient Romans were in many respects quite unlike what we drink today.

It is thus probable that even the earliest grape growers in the Valpolicella—and indeed in other wine producing provinces of the Empire—realized that crushing semi-dried grapes not only gave their wines deeper color and concentration of aromas, but also made it more likely that their product would arrive in reasonable condition to discerning markets further afield.

There are various ways of drying grapes, as the history of dessert wines readily illustrates. In the southern Mediterranean, where winter climates are mild and rain is scarce, the bunches can be late harvested, and then, if necessary, laid out on straw mats in the open air to continue the gradual dehydration process. Each bunch will require daily turning, to ensure that it dries out evenly, but light evening winds and the absence of humidity mean that undesirable molds are not likely to blight the fruit. In more northerly climes, this is generally not the case, and drying must take place indoors.

Some years ago excavation of a Roman villa at Ambrosan, near San Pietro in Cariano in the Valpolicella, brought to light a series of pillared drying rooms dating back to the first to fourth centuries C.E. While in other areas similar structures would have been used for drying out wheat, especially spelt, to stop it germinating, in this district they may well have played a role in appassimento. It was certainly customary for the Romans to heat and smoke casks of wine to speed up the aging process and enhance conservation. This normally took place in the *apothechae*, which were rooms located above the source of heat. However, there were also specially heated cells known as *fumaria* that served the double purpose of warming wine and drying out wood. In mountainous areas a fire was lit in these cells so that fermentation did not stop when the temperature dropped. However, a first century description of winemaking in Marseilles suggests that the practice was also common in the warmer Mediterranean regions.[7]

So it seems reasonable to assume that drying rooms such as those of Ambrosan could have played a role in the production of Verona's famous raisin wine. The Romans often referred to it as Rhaetian wine, after the name of the inhabitants of the Roman province that included the mountainous areas of northern Italy, present day eastern Switzerland and western Austria. Later it was known as *vinum Acinaticium*, on account of the unique property of the grape, or *acinus*, to preserve its color through drying so that crushing in December or January produced juice that was "purple in hue, very sweet, thick and strong."[8] In the nineteenth century the term "Recioto" begins to appear. The name is thought by many to derive from the Latin *racemus*, meaning a small, straggly bunch. It is also suggested that "Recioto" alludes to the shape of the bigger bunches of grapes, which sometimes appear to have "ears" (*recia* in dialect). In Sandro's view, a more convincing derivation is *recisus*, meaning "cut," in relation to the bunches that were cut for drying rather than being left to over-ripen on the vine.

Whatever its origins, the Recioto obtained from grapes dried on cane trays in airy lofts from early October through to early January was generally sweet, because in winter temperatures the transformation of the sugars into alcohol was rarely complete. When, however, the yeasts did manage to carry out their work consistently, the resulting wine would have been dry rather than sweet. The natural antonym of sweet is bitter: *amaro* in Italian, whence Amarone, where the suffix suggests something big. The big, dry/bitter wine was initially differ-

---

7 Martial, x, 36
8 Palladio Rutilio Tauro Emiliano, *De re rustica*.

entiated from its sweeter sibling as Recioto Amaro, and later Recioto Amarone.

Sandro contests the idea that Amarone came into being as a sort of mistake with a positive outcome. "There is plentiful evidence of a preference for the dry version of the wine among discerning palates of the eighteenth century, before the word 'Recioto' even appeared formally," he declares. "By the early 1900s, the term was in fairly common use. We still have a number of pre-World War II Boscaini bottles labeled as 'Recioto Amaro,' made from grapes grown in the Masi vineyards."

The cooperative winery Cantina Sociale Valpolicella bottled a Valpolicella with an additional label on the neck that read Amarone Extra for the 1939 harvest, and a Recioto Amaro Riserva for the 1940 harvest, while Bolla released a Recioto Amarone 1950 in 1953.

For the most part, however, until the 1960s farmers with just a few hectares of vineyard generally set out to make a Recioto. Sandro remembers how his father, Guido, used to be called in for advice when it looked as though excessive fermentation was going to turn the sweet wine "bitter." The expression used for this was *Recioto scapà*—meaning "escaped Recioto." "It was one of the farmer's most feared events, along with hail and when a cow ingested a piece of wire and had to be put down. As far as the Recioto was concerned, my father would tell them to add some sulfur, which halted fermentation, or to rack the wine. But if the transformation of the sugars was almost complete and the wine was already dry, being the merchant that he was my father would suggest buying the wine himself. He knew there was already a market in the restaurants of Verona for what was called '*mezzo recioto*,' which was similar to today's Ripasso."

Once the wines of the Valpolicella were invested with a Denomination of Controlled Origin (DOC) in 1968, the name Recioto remained, with the occasional addition of "Amarone" when the wine was fully fermented. It wasn't until 1991 that some degree of order was introduced, with the recognition of what were effectively two different wines: the sweet Recioto della Valpolicella, and the dry Amarone della Valpolicella. The fame of Amarone had already eclipsed that of its progenitor, acquiring the coveted DOCG status in 2010.

For Amarone as for Recioto, the appassimento process is delicate, complex and remarkable in its effects. The first three weeks or so are the most problematic stage, because the selected bunches need to dry out evenly in the *fruttai*, or lofts. To perform their best, the enzymatic processes within each grape require constant, progressive weight loss, so that they can effect the transformations essential to the development of the aroma, taste and color of the future wine. Here humidity and ventilation play a key role: if the air is too humid and stagnant, undesirable molds can compromise the quality of the grapes, even if the harvest was of exceptionally high quality.

The traditional drying lofts generally have windows on all sides to create cross ventilation that can be controlled to some extent by opening and closing in relation to wind direction. The fruttai higher up the hillside naturally tend to be breezier and less humid, whereas those at a lower altitude can be more challenging. Efforts to speed up and regulate appassimento in artificial environments have not been rewarding. However, a better understanding of many aspects of the process has made it possible to act pre-emptively to avoid damage. Most drying lofts today are equipped with some degree of control equipment, so that losing an entire harvest to gray rot, which used to happen once or twice a decade when appassimento was left entirely in the hands of nature, has now become a rare occurrence. That said, while the new, improved systems ensure that production is possible, they cannot guarantee constant high quality. "The process is a bit like taking a pain-killer for a headache," Sandro points out. "It deals with the symptoms, but doesn't necessarily restore health."

Masi has developed what is probably the most advanced control system for appassimento under the acronym NASA (Natural Serego Super Assisted). The drying room at Gargagnago, at an altitude of 150 meters, is controlled by a computer, which compares the prevailing inside climatic conditions with data derived from all the years in which the climate was judged to be good. If the sensors indicate that the current situation is in line with these parameters, then the conditions in the fruttaio are left in the hands of nature. If, on the other hand, a degree of disparity is shown, then the computer regulates the situation to bring it back to the optimal conditions by closing or opening windows, providing additional ventilation, and so on.

Most winemakers consider their archenemy to be a particular strain of mold called *Botrytis cinerea*, which attacks grape bunches. As the mold takes hold and contributes to desiccation on the vine, the white grapes used for sweet wines will turn golden, then pink or purple, then brown, often with an ash-like powder on the surface: hence the name *cinerea*.

In actual fact, *Botrytis* is not all bad. With classic Venetian curiosity, Masi decided to find out more about it in collaboration with scientists from the University of Verona. They discovered that while *Botrytis* can indeed be a troublemaker, if handled properly it can also make valid contributions to the nascent wine. Much depends on where and when *Botrytis* takes hold.

The causal fungus for bunch rot in the vineyard is appropriately called *Botrytonia fuckelinia*, which brings about the feared gray mildew. This is a particular problem in damp climates, or when there is severe rainfall near harvest, because the spores germinate on wet surfaces and in high ambient humidity. When *Botrytis* behaves badly, it produces such gray rot. In its benevolent form, however, when early morning autumn mists are followed by warm, sunny afternoons, *Botrytis* can perform a small miracle known as noble rot. This it does by penetrating the skins of ripe grapes with filaments that leave minute brown spots on the skin, making it impenetrable by other harmful micro-organisms. *Botrytis cinerea* consumes the sugar in the grapes, but is far more voracious with the acids, so the overall effect is greater concentration of sugars and a velvety quality produced by glycerol and gluconic acid.

Noble rot in a vineyard growing grapes for dessert wines is one thing; its role in the drying rooms of the Valpolicella is another, and relates to the desired style of the Amarone. A greater degree of *Botrytis*, and thus of glycerol, will make the wine more fiery, rounded, velvety and full-bodied, with intense aromas of overripe fruit or fruit preserved in spirit. Less or no *Botrytis* will produce more austere wines with greater tannic structure. Obviously the aging potential and the maturation curve vary according to the chosen style of wine. Of the three grape varieties that are traditionally used for Amarone, Corvina is the most vulnerable to noble rot, which causes it to lose fruit and color, but gain in roundedness. The most recent studies undertaken by the Masi Technical Group have shown that while Rondinella is much less subject to *Botrytis* because of its thick, dark skins, the development of glycerol that does come about is proportionally much higher. *Botrytis* also attacks the light red Molinara variety, which features as a small percentage in the blend.

The laws governing Amarone production dictate that appassimento should continue through to at least December 15. Masi extends this period to the second half of January, by which time the grapes will have lost thirty-five to forty percent of their weight. Apart from the concentration of sugars, aromas, colors and tannins, and the additional smoothness that comes with *Botrytis*, protracted drying in controlled environments also promotes the development of greater complexity.

When the grapes are ready for crushing, they will be partially or totally removed from the stems, which by this time are completely dry. Because of the low temperatures, fermentation in the winter is preceded by natural cold maceration that lasts for around two weeks, during which the skins release substances that enrich the must with fresh, fruity aromas, and the pulp supplies the yeasts responsible for fermentation with nutrients. Further maceration takes place during fermentation, and in this phase the anthocyanins, or flavonoid pigments present in the fruit, are released into the must, thereby fixing the color through their reaction with the tannins and increasing aromatic complexity with the aid of the alcohol and other substances created by the yeasts during fermentation. This latter maceration may last from twenty five to forty days, in relation to climate and other variables.[9]

At this point the wine is racked, or taken off the lees, though it is still essentially sweet. Transferred into large oak casks, the wine feels the effects of spring and with the addition of selected yeasts completes the transformation of sugars into alcohol, giving birth to Amarone.

Fifty years ago, natural alcoholic fermentation brought about by yeasts naturally present in the grapes was a somewhat hit-and-miss affair in winter, because low temperatures often put the sugar-devouring micro-organisms out of action for several days or weeks, leaving the half-fermented must in a somewhat vulnerable hiatus. Today the phenomenon is better understood and easier to control, thanks to the identification and selection of a particular strain of yeast that carries out its work consistently and without interruption: *Saccharomices bayanus.* There is also a secondary fermentation, which is more elusive and difficult to control. This is malolactic fermentation that is brought about by certain strains of lactic bacteria, in particular *Oenoccus oeni,* which transform the malic acid naturally present in new wines to lactic acid, thereby decreasing the perception of the overall acidity of the wine. Malolactic fermentation enhances complexity, investing Amarone with an almost buttery smoothness and bringing out notes of spice and dried fruit.

Greater understanding of how the different grapes react during appassimento, and what these transformations impart to Amarone, has led the Masi team to take a look at other grape varieties and their behavior when crushed and fermented semi-dried. Speaking at a seminar organized by the Society of Wine Educators in 2000, Sandro Boscaini summed up the winery's experiments with making an unorthodox Amarone. The aim was to see whether they could create a new version of the wine

---

9 Detailed accounts of these and related processes can be found in Lanfranco Paronetto's various contributions to the Technical Seminars organized by Masi at Vinitaly in Verona, for instance, "*Appassimento—Nuove sensazioni nel mondo,* 2002."

that might have more appeal for the international consumer. "Our efforts revolved around the selection of non-traditional varieties, which in time were whittled down to four: Oseleta, Sangiovese Grosso, Cabernet Sauvignon and Raboso Veronese. They underwent exactly the same drying process used for Corvina, Rondinella and Molinara, and were then vinified separately. A series of tasting events were organized with the Swiss wine magazine *Vinum*. Participants were provided with glass measuring jars and five sample wines made from semi-dried grapes: a classic Amarone blend of Corvina, Molinara and Rondinella; an Oseleta; a Raboso Veronese; a Sangiovese Grosso; and a Cabernet Sauvignon. The idea was that people could revise the traditional Amarone, or create their own blend. Well, the amazing thing was that practically everyone came to the conclusion that the classic blend could simply not be bettered. Of course, that's what history has also told us—but we needed to find out whether tradition and value really do coincide. And we discovered to our gratification that there was no room left for doubt."

Aging well

Once the fermentation processes are over, the nascent wine is ready to mature quietly in wooden casks that will help it achieve its full potential in a number of different ways. The rules pertaining to Amarone production establish two years as the minimum duration for aging, though many producers choose to extend this considerably.

The porous nature of the wood allows for a slow, continuous dissolution of minute amounts of oxygen in the wine, which provokes certain reactions, including the stabilization of color, which tends towards a slightly darker hue, and the evolution of taste and aroma. The main oxidizable compounds in wine are phenolics, which include wine pigments. This form of microoxidation also creates other useful compounds that are more resistant to further, undesirable oxidation of the sort that could turn the color brownish and compromise the fruitiness of a wine like Amarone, making it flat and slightly sherry-like.

While it reposes in casks, the wine gradually deposits the suspended particles in the form of sediment. However, the wood also imparts something of its own to the wine, including numerous aromatic compounds, tannins and phenolics that derive from its own origins, the treatment it has undergone and its age. To give of its best, the wood requires a certain temperature and level of humidity. In the case of Amarone, the temperature should not go above 10° C (50°F)in the autumn following production, so that the precipitation of sediment is completed in a relatively short time. From the second year, the wine is kept at around 12–15° C (53.6–59°F). As for humidity, a lack dries out the liquid too fast, while too much can damage the wood. The ideal middle ground is between 75 and 85% humidity.

Wooden casks come in a wide variety of sizes, from the truly gigantic to the relatively Lilliputian barrique, though not many producers of Amarone have chosen to squeeze their gentle giants into such cramped quarters. While the Masi cellars at Gargagnago comprise an enormous 500-hectoliter barrel that is built *in situ* and measures 4.5 meters in height and 4.40 in width, the winery's chosen cask has long been the *fusto veronese*, a 600 liter barrel made from French or Slavonian oak. Because of its manageable size, this particular type of container was once used for transporting wine, which traveled on boats down the Adige River towards the Adriatic Sea, and from here to a number of cities by ship, or on carts, and later trucks, heading towards Milan and Switzerland. When used for aging wines, these casks have a useful lifespan of about five to six years, after which they become essentially passive containers. Once upon a time, the *fusto veronese* was generally made with wood sourced in the vicinity, which tended to be chestnut or cherry. Out of respect for this tradition, the Serego Alighieri red wines are still partly aged in 600-liter cherrywood casks, but only for a period of three to four months, which is long enough to impart particular aromas. Longer aging in porous woods of this sort could encourage unwelcome oxidation.

With careful selection in the vineyard and greater control of conditions during appassimento, maceration and fermentation, a modern Amarone is already enjoyable to drink three or four years after harvest. Yet its potential extends well beyond such timelines, unfolding like the narrative fabric of an intriguing epic novel. Amarone evolves in two different stages. The first extends to the eleventh year after harvest, or sometimes slightly beyond, during which time the quality of the wine continues to evolve in terms of structure, youthful exuberance, powerful aromas and flavors of raisined fruit. During the second stage, the wine loses its original fruity character, acquiring hints of aromatic herbs that are emphasized by the high alcohol level and become more refined and elegant. On the nose, rich, spicy perfumes come to the fore, almost oriental in impact. On the palate, the wine is intense, elegant and velvety, with smooth tannins and a rich aftertaste ending with a hint of licorice.

Masi produces five Amarones, which makes it the foremost giant tamer in the Valpolicella. Three of these wines are *crus*, meaning that each is the expression of a single vineyard, from which it derives its distinctive traits. Campolongo di Torbe can rightly claim pride of place among these highly individual wines, originating as it does from the eponymous vineyard located in the Torbe district of Negrar, at an altitude that ranges from 375 to 400 meters (1,230–1,300 feet) above sea level. The vineyard faces southwest, the vine rows are aligned north-to-south, and the reddish soils consist largely of Eocene limestone. Overlooking the terraced vineyard like a massive, benevolent guardian is a curious mound of volcanic origin. Fragments of the same basalt intermixed with the soil are what accounts for the distinctive nature of this supremely elegant Amarone: the hint of bitter almond and cherrystone that is present in the bouquet, and lingers on the palate.

The second cru is the Mazzano Amarone, which comes from the other estate identified in the twelfth century as a superb winegrowing area by the bibulous monks of San Zeno. Located at an altitude of 350–415 meters, the west-facing Mazzano vineyard is one of the highest in the Valpolicella. Deeply sloping and terraced with dry-stone walls, the rows of vines follow the curve of the terrain in their northeast-southwest alignment, nurtured by soils composed of brown Cretaceous marl. Appassimento takes place in drying lofts on the property, with the grapes laid out exclusively on bamboo racks until pressing, usually in the second half of January. The resulting wine has great depth and structure, marrying slightly austere nobility with gentle tannins and velvety elegance. Little wonder that Jancis Robinson, the doyenne of British wine writers, described it as "perhaps the truest, and certainly the highest, vineyard for Valpolicella's oddity called Amarone."[10]

In terms of historic renown, Masi's third cru is just as impressive as the previous two; indeed, perhaps more so. The grapes that produce Vaio Armaron come from a small valley of the same name located in the Gargagnago district of Sant'Ambrogio, between 190 and 265 meters above sea level. One of the most prestigious *cru* sites of the Valpolicella Classica, it belongs to the Serego Alighieri estate. While the vineyard faces southwest, the actual rows of vines are variously orientated, following the lie of the land. The soils are light brown and friable, of average depth with little organic matter. Appassimento takes place in the drying lofts at the Serego Alighieri villa, with the grapes laid to dry partially on bamboo racks and partially in trays until pressing in January. This is Masi's most traditional Amarone, in the sense that its kinship to Recioto is subtly recognizable. The bouquet is complex and inviting, with aromas of overripe cherry and cooked plums, while in the mouth the initial impact of sweetness gives way to plenty of cherry and ripe berries, with a hint of cinnamon and vanilla.

While the Costasera Amarone is not a cru, in that the grapes are sourced from several hillsides, it has a coherence that led Bengt-Goran Kronstam of the Swedish paper *Dagens Nyheter* to pronounce it "one of the best taste examples in the world of this kind of wine. The reason," he explained, "is that it does not 'lose its focus,' but keeps its sharpness despite huge concentration. To create something big is not difficult in the

---

10 Jancis Robinson, *Vintage Time Charts*, London, Weidenfeld & Nicholson, 1989

wine world, but the finesse is much more difficult."[11] What these different hillsides share is the fact that they face southwest, enjoying the sun's rays through to sunset and the extra light reflected from Lake Garda. So favorable a position is like the kiss of fortune, making the wine fruity and approachable. Costasera is an Amarone that respects tradition, but also answers the contemporary demand for wines that can be served with food. It is a Titan with a soft voice and charming manner.

The Riserva di Costasera is a *cuvee* of the same origins, with the addition of a small percentage of semi-dried Oseleta, which confers great tannic structure and deeper color. Appassimento is extended to at least 120 days, and long aging in 600-liter Slavonian and Allier oak casks blends the initial aromas of jam and berries with a distinct note of black pepper and nutmeg. Though the wine is huge, intense and full-bodied, it has a remarkably fresh finish. Italians would call it a *vino da pasto*, but also a *vino da divano*.[12]

Despite their different natures, the Masi giants share a family trait: approachability. This is even the case with the Mazzano Amarone, the most austere, or the least baroque, member of the brood. It is intriguing, beguiling, fulfilling—the sort of wine you feel you should not only savor, but pay all-around attention to. "Amarone is a natural top-of-the-list wine," declares Sandro Boscaini with characteristic dry humor. "It begins with an 'A,' which places it before Italy's other famous wines, many of which begin with a 'B.' But for all its immediate visibility, it doesn't allow for head-on acquaintance. It's too rounded and elusive. I think that to appreciate Amarone to the full requires all five senses. Taste and smell are obvious contenders, and so is sight, from our perception of the vineyards bathed in gentle sunlight to the deep, dense red of the wine itself. But that is not all. When the grapes are drying out they take on unexpected tactile qualities, and the wine in the mouth has a tangible vel-

---

11 Bengt-Goran Kronstam, *Dagens Nyheter*, Sweden, December 6, 2009
12 A wine for food, or the sofa.

vety body not found to the same degree in other reds. As for our sense of hearing, if you listen carefully, appassimento is full of micro-sounds as the grapes change shape during dehydration, and the movement that accompanies fermentation also creates a quiet, vibrant sort of music that's almost hypnotic. Once you're aware of this breadth of experience it comes naturally to approach the wine as you would a sort of legendary hero who actually turns out to be easy to converse with, soft-spoken and learned, but never pompous or self-important. We like to think of our Valpolicella giants as sensuous beings of great all-around stature and appeal."

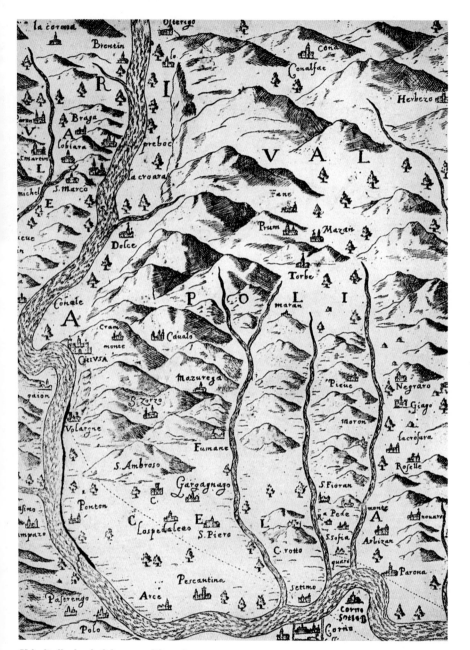

Valpolicella, land of Amarone. Map, 1625

The valley is protected by the Alpine foothills to the north, which account for the mild temperature

Cherrytrees flowering in spring

The steep slopes of Mazzano in autumn

The magnificent Corno d'Aquilio mountain towering over the surrounding fields

The Ponte di Veja, a natural bridge-like rock formation

The gentle slopes of Gargagnago, with the Masi and Serego Alighieri vineyards

The visual harmony of vines, cypress trees and olive groves at San Ciriaco

Sergio and Sandro Boscaini

Sandro as a young man on a trip to Holland

Pater Familias Guido Boscaini and his family

Diploma for excellence in Oenology awarded to Sandro's grandfather Paolo in 1931

The Boscaini family at Masi today: Raffaele, Alessandra, Sandro, Bruno and Mario.

The Masi Technical Group, when it was founded in 1979 . . .

. . . and today.

The Boscaini house at Valgatara, late 18th century. It has been the centre of the family's life and activities since 1888

Villa Serego Alighieri at Gargagnago. The property along with surrounding vineyards was purchased by Pietro, the son of the poet Dante Alighieri, in 1353

Harvest scenes in the Serego Alighieri vineyards. Drawing c. 1700; photograph 1921.

Vines trained to the Guyot system on the hillside at San Ciriaco

Grape harvest in the Campolongo vineyard at Torbe

Corvina Veronese, the queen of the Amarone grapes

(and 22b) Rondinella and Molinara, the other two varieties that join with Corvina in the classic Amarone blend

Oseleta, an ancient grape variety that has been rediscovered by Masi

The delicate process of leaving bunches of grapes to semi-dry slowly on cane trays known as 'arele'

The traditional barn, or 'fruttaio', at Mazzano, used for semi-drying the grapes. 1950s

A modern version of the 'fruttaio' used for semi-drying the grapes at Gargagnago, where temperature and humidity are controlled by the NASA (Natural Serego Super Assisted) system

Bruce Schoenfeld once declared that Boscaini is to Amarone what Gaja is to Barbaresco and Antinori to Chianti.

The small miracle of noble rot on semi-dried grapes

The drying rooms at Serego Alighieri, with the grapes undergoing 'appassimento' in the cold of winter

Crushing the semi-dried grapes and removing the stalks

First racking the Amarone, which still contains plenty of residual sugar.

The traditional cellars at the original Boscaini home, 1950s

Ageing the wine in wood at Gargagnago. During this process the Amarone gradually becomes dry

The traditional Veronese casks for ageing the wine contain 620 liters

Amarone undergoing bottle ageing

*Costasera, where the
hillsides glow in the
warmth of the evening sun
Masi's Costasera, a modern
wine with an ancient heart*

Riserva di Costasera Masi, an Amarone that links past with future

The oldest Serego Alighieri bottle, which dates back to 1672

Past vintages of Amarone Masi

Vaio Armaron Serego Alighieri: the complex, mysterious nature of a 'gentle giant', as Wine Spectator called it

According to Burton Anderson, Campofiorin Masi created a new category of Veronese wines

Enjoy Amarone to its fullest, with the right glass, the right temperature . . . and the right company

Mazzano and Campolongo di Torbe are Masi wines that give voice to different terroirs

The barrel signed at the Premio Masi Awards, when Amarone promotes culture

Pierre Cardin, one of the prize–winners in 1997

Philippine de Rothschild with Piero Antinori, 1996

Luciano Benetton, who was awarded the Masi Prize in 1986

Interest in Amarone: Bill Gates visiting Villa Serego Alighieri

Friendship through Amarone: Sandro and Paolo Roberto

Milo Manara's interpretation of Civiltà veneta, or Venetian Civilization

IV

IDENTITY

I t is not unusual for the seeds of some of life's more positive developments to be sown when a few friends get
together to enjoy a drink in a relaxed atmosphere. What takes
place is the opposite of brainstorming, and arguably more effective. Instead of spurring the gray matter into overdrive, an
agreeable beverage in good company can quiet the mind, helping it cast off the superfluous and reflect on what is essential.

Thirty years ago, Sandro Boscaini was enjoying a glass of
wine with a couple of old friends at the Bottega del Vino, a
historic watering hole in Verona. Founded in 1890, this tavern
had long been a favorite meeting place for the local intelli-
gentsia as well as for Veronese winemakers. In those days, the
Boscainis supplied the cellars with casks of the Valpolicella
red. Today Masi produces some of the best-loved bottles in a
wine list that has grown to become one of Italy's finest. The
cuisine has also expanded, providing the right gastronomic
partnership for such enological prominence. Yet the Bottega
del Vino has remained true to its original vocation as a home
from home for many Veronesi, from wine producers and busi-
nessmen to local residents. Indeed, it serves pensioners who
while away the day over a glass of wine and a meatball with the
same grace it reserves for wine critics and captains of industry drawn by the promise of an excellent lunch washed down

with something special. In this it epitomizes a certain spirit of the Veneti: at the same time busy but welcoming, relaxed but professional.

Little wonder, then, that Sandro unconsciously picked the Bottega del Vino as a venue for reflecting on his regional identity. That evening he found himself telling his friends about his perception of being Venetian. Travel throughout Europe, the USA and Japan had made him aware of how small, and indeed insignificant, the Veneto was in many people's eyes. And it had come as a bit of a shock. "The Veneti usually believe their provenance to be something akin to a sign of nobility," he admitted ruefully. "In actual fact, we're often considered complete provincials, because for decades the region has been so poor. In the wine business, for instance, growers like myself have never enjoyed the recognition reserved for the Tuscans or the Piedmontese. In general the Veneto is known for cheap wines, and I find this very disappointing. I'm educated, I've travelled the world, and I'm proud of my family's roots as winemakers. I'm also convinced of the great potential of our wines, but in the overall picture something's always missing."

"Then why don't you seek out other Venetians who share your belief in the importance of our cultural roots and origins?", suggested his old friend Cesare Marchi, raising his glass. Firmly attached to his hometown of Villafranca di Verona, Marchi was a well-known journalist, writer and television personality who had never been lured away to live in Milan or Rome, where most of his colleagues resided. The other member of the congenial trio was Nini (Giovanni) Vicentini, a journalist and author with a perceptive focus on the region of his birth. Vicentini agreed that Sandro should act on his intuition. A mine of information on local customs, the writer had great faith in the *genius loci* of the Veneto. In fact he regaled his companions with an account of a curious Veronese observance: in earlier times, when men got together to drink wine, before raising the glass to their lips they would dip two fingers into the wine and let drops fall to the ground in a propitiatory gesture to Mother Earth. There was a lesson to be learned from this. The winemakers of the Veneto, he declared, should express pride in local viticulture and belief in the persistent creative spirit of their land.

The terrain was fertile, and the seed of Sandro's reflections began to germinate. The three friends talked about the possibility of establishing an award for Venetian identity, a prize for belief in roots and the ability to enhance the heritage of the Veneto for future generations. "Better to recognize and reward these values while people are still alive than to write a fine obituary once they're dead," remarked Cesare Marchi with characteristic aplomb. "But what should the award consist of?" "A barrel of Amarone," Sandro replied without hesitation. "After all, apart from being delectable, a glass of wine helps you understand the connection with the land. It reflects our civilization, its myths, rites and culture."

Over the next few months, Sandro and his friends thought long and hard about what differentiated the spirit of the Veneto from that of other regions of Italy. Clearly the historical role of Venice as a gateway for exchange with the East played a major part in the overall picture. The Venetian seafarers of bygone days were driven not only by the promise of mercantile gain, but also by the desire to find out what lay beyond the horizon. Manuscripts of the sixteenth and seventeenth centuries reveal a constant curiosity for the systems that prevailed in distant lands, a sense of engagement that transcended the primary desire to secure supplies or locate markets for Venetian goods.

To add to this, there was the sheer inventiveness implicit in a city built on small islands in a lagoon: an expanse of water that mirrored the changing humors of the sky, but protected the city from the tumult of the wider sea beyond. Similar creative flair was also evident in the work of artists whose paintings revealed unprecedented skill in handling light. In their different ways, Titian, Tintoretto, Veronese and Tiepolo all made use of vibrant colors that define shape and suggest movement to portray the shimmer of rippled water, the luminescence of youthful complexion or the rich sheen of a silken gown.

It is tempting to believe that an awareness of light might naturally lead to enlightenment. Certainly the attitude of the

Venetian Republic towards the cities of the terra firma spoke for farsighted conviction that dialogue was always more fruitful than enmity and conflict. Venice could dominate without domineering. To be a dominion was a form of allegiance, not a disenfranchisement. Such reflections were evidently in the air during the early 1980s, as Mikhail Gorbachov's pursuit of *glasnost* (openness) and *perestroika* (restructuring) sowed the seeds for change in the contours of Eastern Europe.

That meeting so appropriately hosted at the Bottega del Vino ultimately developed into the Premio Masi Civiltà Veneta, an annual award for Venetian civilization inaugurated in 1981. Sandro worried for a while about whether the name Masi should actually feature at all. Did it smack of self-promotion of the chest-beating variety? Of un-Venetian braggadocio? In the end he came to the conclusion that rewarding excellence with Amarone simply showed that the winery was as happy with its own products as it was proud of the achievements of outstanding Venetians.

Cesare Marchi was one of the original board members of the Premio Masi, while Nini Vicentini took on the role of Secretary, and later also of editor of the acts of the award proceedings. Other prominent people in various fields also took part, and many of them are still involved in the initiative. The first chairman of the Jury was Vittore Branca, the great philologist and literary critic who was born in Liguria, but became Professor Emeritus of Italian literature at the University of Padua. He was succeeded by Feliciano Benvenuti, a professor of law born in Padua who later became Vice Chancellor of the University of Venice. A man of great and widespread learning, his many publications included judicial, historical, political and social studies. Both had travelled widely, taught in a great number of learned institutions across the globe, and received various degrees *honoris causa* and other attestations of merit at home and abroad. Yet both also looked forward to the congenial quarterly Jury meetings, discussing potential award candidates with a typically Venetian touch of humor. "I was both surprised and flattered that such eminent personalities were happy to come on board," Sandro admits. "It made me feel that my project really was worthwhile. I also think that having Amarone as the symbol and matrix of the prize rang especially true to them."

In the course of time, additions were made to the original format of the award. The prize for Venetian civilization was accompanied in 1987 by another prize that recognized a particular contribution to wine culture anywhere in the world: the Premio Masi Civiltà del Vino. Moreover, by the turn of the Millennium it was becoming clear that running what had become a major cultural venture should be entrusted to a specially set-up foundation, thereby separating it institutionally from the winery as such. The perfect opportunity arose with the twentieth anniversary of the Prize, when the then-Chairman, Demetrio Volcic, a well-known TV personality and writer on geopolitics, launched the Fondazione Masi. Within a few months of its inception in 2001, the Board of Governors agreed that there was still one important aspect of the Venetian heritage that was as yet unrecognized: the ability to reach out, to build bridges, to encourage exchange and thereby eradicate potential conflict. Thus the Premio Grosso d'Oro Veneziano came into being, in recognition of what can perhaps best be described as farsighted diplomacy. It takes the shape of a gold medal replicating the Grosso coin that was legal tender for several centuries not only within the dominions of the Republic, but also in a wide area of Central Europe and the Eastern Mediterranean. The first person to receive this award was Milan Kucan, who steered the newly founded Republic of Slovenia through its peaceful transition from vassal of Yugoslavia into an independent, modern state open to exchange with the neighboring nations of Italy, Austria, Hungary and Croatia.

The celebration of these particular accomplishments has grown in scope and participation over the decades. The early editions took place in the beautiful Romanesque church of San Giorgio in Valpolicella, overlooking a landscape of terraced vineyards and olive groves towards Lake Garda. Clearly there was symbolic value in this choice of venue, since San Giorgio was the religious and cultural center for the Arusnati, the original inhabitants of the Valpolicella. With the growth of the prize, however, San Giorgio was no longer able to accommodate all the guests, so another significant auditorium was chosen in its stead: the historic Teatro Filarmonico in Verona.

Despite the august nature of both of these institutions, there is nothing pompous or self-congratulatory about the Premio Masi—that would simply be out of character. The prevailing atmosphere was perfectly summed up by the conductor Claudio Scimone, founder of the Solisti Veneti chamber orchestra that won the award for Venetian Civilization in 1982. "It's not just that the Prize corresponds to a program that's important as far as our lives and our careers are concerned," the musician declared. "There's a leitmotif in the way it's all managed and the nature of the prize-giving that reveals a subtle but distinct touch of humor."

It is probably true that you need a touch of humor to recognize it in others. But then Claudio Scimone, who was born in Padua, is as Venetian as they come. As a regional trait, this humor is a smile rather than a belly laugh, a quizzical nod rather than a guffaw. It's only to be expected that the Bacchic masks on display at the Archeological Museum by the Roman Theater in Verona should reveal a happy countenance. But even San Zeno, the fourth century patron saint of Verona, is traditionally depicted with a smile on his face.

For Sandro Boscaini, the quiet smile of the Veneto has to do with a feeling of self-confidence, an assuredness that has its roots in shared history. "It doesn't suggest that we think we can go out and conquer the world. It's more that we really do know our own products and are convinced that they will be appreciated elsewhere as well. This gives us the strength to propose things, without wishing to impose them."

Language

All areas of the Venetian Republic shared a common language, the slightly singsong dialect that Venetians of all backgrounds still gladly slip into amongst themselves. It has a distinguished history. During the mid-1700s, the great playwright Carlo Goldoni, well-versed in linguistic nicety through his original training as a lawyer, penned a hugely popular series of comedies that renewed a theatrical tradition in which improvisation had hitherto held sway. In committing the lines of each of the actors to paper, Goldoni opted for a mixture of Italian and the Venetian dialect that invested both with value. Human foibles were his recurrent themes, expressed in the language of the people who flocked to enjoy his works.

The fame of these brilliant comedies spread well beyond the sphere of influence of the Venetian Republic. In 1762, Goldoni was invited to Paris, where he was involved in promoting the Italian theater he had helped reform, and teaching Italian to the daughters of Louis XV. He continued to write, both for the Parisian stage and for theatrical companies back in Venice, enjoying a court pension until the Revolution put an end to such royally conferred privileges.

While theaters in other cities of the Italian peninsula were founded by or relied on the patronage of the aristocracy, in Venice they had long been run as potentially profitable enterprises. Goldoni wrote for professional companies managed by impresarios connected with particular theaters that vied with others for custom. He recognized the commercial as well as the cultural value of the printed word, and wrote for the widest possible audience. The fact that his plays mirrored the comedy of daily life rather than focusing on its darker sides speaks for an attitude that may also be characteristic of the Veneto: a propensity for reconciling art with business in the name of enjoyment.

It is thus perhaps no coincidence that the printed word was the main focus of the first edition of the Premio Masi. The prize was awarded to Biagio Marin, the patriarch of Venetian poetry; to the novelist Elio Bertolini, a native of Friuli; to Alvise Zorzi for his lifelong devotion to introducing a wider readership to the history of Venice; and to journalist Giulio Nascimbeni, whose articles in the *Corriere della Sera* newspaper always showed depth of analysis and elegance of form.

Sandro has described Biagio Marin and Alvise Zorzi as two paradigms of the Venetian identity that complete each other. The patrician Zorzi was the more sophisticated of the two, a man of great culture and bearing, impeccable in his elegance in a way that transcends mere physical aspect. Though fluent in a number of languages, Zorzi is the sort of Venetian who happily returns to his native dialect whenever he finds himself with fellow Venetians. Biagio Marin, by contrast, came from a very poor family from Grado, at the top end of the Adriatic. "He was an extraordinary person, ninety years old and practically blind, but in his own way a visionary. His poetry was full of feeling, like familiar sounds rather than words. You could tell that Marin's verse sprang from generations of experience, from his surroundings, with the water and canals and wide stretches of marshy land full of bird life. His creativity was like a vegetable that flourishes in certain soils. He used dialect and onomatopoeia to wonderful, lyrical effect, expressing universal truths. I blame my own laziness that my children never got to meet him. He was a man of great insight, almost a prophet."

In a note written not long before his death, Marin recalled how as a child he was taught the French expression *noblesse oblige*, which he understood as meaning that nobility implies obligations, such as discipline, duty and style: "We must at least have style, because we belong to this wonderful community of the Veneti, who have given so much to art ... Art means humanity raised to the realms of the divine. Art is divinity, spirituality; it's about leaving the man-beast plane for the ideal sphere, the sphere of the spirit and creativity."

In later years, the ranks of outstanding Venetians swelled to include musicians, museum directors, actors, designers, sculptors, economists and industrialists, all of whom exemplified the mixture of energy, foresight and outreach that Sandro, Cesare and Nini had recognized as characteristic of their region at its best. Whatever their provenance or profession, however, language is arguably the most important common thread linking them to their past.

Writer Isabella Bossi Fedrigotti, who won the Premio Masi in 1995 and since 2009 has taken over the chairmanship of the Fondazione, has described what the Venetian dialect means to her in characteristically thoughtful, limpid terms: "Dialect is what I love best of the Veneto," she recently declared. "It feels familiar because it's so close to what we speak in the Trentino. I love the way it has resisted change. Language takes on new words and foreign terms, whereas dialect remains true to itself, both sweet and rough, ironic and melancholy, apparently capable only of referring to basic everyday things of home, land or sea, but in actual fact able to express the ineffable, to explain what is subtle, elevated and indescribable." She then went on to suggest that in times of rapid change, when people feel they've lost their bearings, a familiar dialect can be reassuring, suggest direction, act as a refuge. "When you hear someone from the Veneto speaking in Italian," she added, "you get the impression he's translating from his own rich, secret language into an official idiom that's a bit stiff and formal, and not nearly as fecund."

Another novelist to win the Premio Masi Civiltà Veneta is Susanna Tamaro, author of *Follow Your Heart* and *Answer Me*, which have enjoyed widespread international acclaim. When she received the award in 2002, Tamaro added a telling personal reflection to the subject of dialect, which she views as an integral part of the landscape. She described how she left her native Trieste at the age of eighteen, convinced that the prevailing concept of duty played a stultifying role in the lives of those born and bred there. Instead she chose to live in Rome, which she perceived as cynical, unchanging, indifferent to its own ineluctable decline, but devoted to pleasure. The former was the Veneto, at least historically; the latter, with its sun and palm trees, Italy.

Needless to say, as soon as she took up residence in the capital, her newfound freedom hung heavily around her, and she suffered from tremendous waves of homesickness for the beautiful city that connected north with south, east with west. Whenever she could, she bought a train ticket and headed for home. On reaching Mestre, the mainland junction across the water from Venice, she would feel her heart lighten and her spirits revive as she took in the familiar rows of poplars, the farmhouses, and the dialect of the inhabitants. "There are certain landscapes that can shape a person's character," she declared, "shape it and devastate it. But as the years slip by I have come to realize that what I thought was devastation was in fact a form of sensible stability, the ability to work consistently without paying attention to the surrounding confusion. This turned out to be my salvation, maintaining the spirit of the northeast while living in the midst of deep-rooted Mediterranean inertia."

The Venetian dialect can become distinctly tangible. Sandro would argue that Amarone is a form of liquid dialect that is distinctive, quite unlike that of the Mediterranean or indeed other parts of northern Italy. "The wine has a style of its own, and other inimitable features that make it an expression of place. In actual fact it's a great example of what goes by the name of 'glocal,' meaning proudly local, and for this reason able to make its presence felt on the global market."

Industry

The Veneti take particular pleasure in doing things well. They are scrupulous in their attention to detail, ready to innovate rather than to repeat what has already been done, and inclined to imbue their products with individuality. In other words, they are remarkably industrious. Yet their vocation as industrialists is relatively recent. During the nineteenth and early twentieth centuries, poverty was so widespread that for many people emigration became the only hope for survival. From 1861, when the region became part of the new kingdom of a united Italy, more people emigrated from the Veneto over the following hundred years than from any other Italian region, including Sicily and Calabria. Furthermore, the trend continued until relatively late. Between 1951 and 1960, an average of 40,000 people, largely men, were leaving the region each year, many of them heading for Brazil and Argentina. Their renown for implacable perseverance and fortitude soon spread abroad, making them welcome as laborers. And they created, in their adoptive lands, associations and communities that preserved their shared dialect and cultural traditions.

So when in the mid-1980s Sandro's desire to recognize and reward the spirit of the Veneto expanded its focus to include captains of industry, he was making a point that had hitherto eluded most outside observers: the Veneto was changing, investing in new approaches to products and production that within two decades would transform it from an economic backwater to Italy's most successful region as regards employment, GDP and exports.

In 1983 the Masi prize was awarded to Pietro Marzotto, head of a historic family textile manufacturing company located near Vicenza. Three years later, prominent members of two other family industries from the Veneto received the award: Luciano Benetton, whose brand of brightly colored knitwear gave a fun new look to clothing stores and made fashion available to a much wider public; and Luciano Vistosi, who had enabled a traditional glassmaking company on the island of Murano to flank one-off pieces with small-scale serial production thanks to the introduction of contemporary design and improved manufacturing techniques.

Marzotto, Benetton and Vistosi represent three very different aspects of Venetian enterprise. Founded in 1836, Marzotto had grown into a large concern that comprised seven textile factories and, by the early 1980s, employed six thousand people. It stood for tradition, textiles being the one factory system that provided an alternative to subsistence farming in the Veneto during the nineteenth and early twentieth century. Benetton, on the other hand, totally overturned the traditional manufacturing system, subcontracting out the different stages of garment production, initially knitwear, to smaller, independent companies who were supplied with the materials and agreed to precise delivery schedules. Hitherto, knitwear manufacturers had worked with colored yarns. Benetton broke new ground by dyeing the garments once they were finished, which allowed the company to feel the pulse of the market and thus ride confidently on the crest of any fashion wave. It was the triumph of advanced planning, logistics and distribution. As for Vistosi, the company spoke for that quintessential Venetian approach to creativity, interweaving contemporary design with the skill of traditional craftsmen to produce beautiful objects for a much wider audience.

In some respects, Masi itself embodies a little of each of these different entrepreneurial threads, interwoven with a fourth that is typical of Italian industry in general, but particularly so of production in the Veneto. The winery shares with Marzotto a claim to historical continuity. In other words, as a family business that dates back a good eight generations, it has witnessed and contributed to the changes that account for the region's newfound prosperity. With Benetton it has in common forms of collaboration between smaller businesses and the brand company that require a dynamic system of management and logistics. In Masi's case, this means the independent growers who sell their grapes to Masi, in accordance with ongoing viticultural input from the Masi Technical Group. Another similar feature is the innovative approach to communication that both companies have long realized is essential to commercial success. What Oliviero Toscani has done for the clothing label with his photographs illustrating "The United Colors of Benetton" is to establish brand recognition. In a quieter way, and on a smaller scale, Masi has brought about the same visibility for its products not only by the visual impact of labels, but also by organizing and hosting important scientific debate at Vinitaly, keeping customers up to date with the Masi Flash newsletter, and reaching out to new audiences through events such as the Premio Masi.

Yet it is with Luciano Vistosi that Masi arguably has the greatest analogies. For Vistosi is also a firm whose products speak for artisanal expertise and accomplishment, and at the same time for the promise of consistency in production of the highest quality. It's a question of marrying the knowhow of past generations with select technical improvements. When this is translated into winemaking, it means the ability to produce commercially relevant quantities of bottles that are both highly individual, yet reliably constant. "We're not interested in the kind of exclusiveness that means buyers come begging for a bottle or two, which are so few and far between that they become a sort of fetish," Sandro declares. "Our output is a bit like the production of art multiples, where what underpins repeatability is quality and house style."

The fourth trait typical of industry in the Veneto, and to some degree also present in the Masi winery, revolves around what in Italian goes by the name of a *distretto*. This is the concentration in a particular area of a cluster of small firms with a common manufacturing focus and a high degree of specialization. The Veneto boasts some fifteen of these *distretti*, comprising 10,000 firms that employ over 100,000 people. The printing industry, textiles, fashion, construction, chemicals and food are just some of the product sectors that have found organizational support and commercial leverage through belonging to such a cluster.

This approach to manufacture is often referred to as "widespread entrepreneurship." Within such a system, each operator is his or her own master and has such faith in his product that he tends to view institutions such as the Chamber of Commerce with diffidence. "That used to be pretty much my attitude as well," Sandro admits. "But in time I realized that if bureaucratic organizations of this sort are left in the hands of people lacking experience or vision, they can actually be quite damaging. I'm not saying this is intentional. It's simply that people with desk jobs don't depend on actually having to go out and sell a product, which means they don't always see the implications of their actions. So I now believe it's important to monitor their policies, trying to make a concrete contribution that derives from our experience of production and knowledge of the market. That's why I'm currently involved in various national and local associations regarding the wine sector. While winegrowing in the Valpolicella doesn't officially come into the cluster category, premium producers have come up against plenty of this sort of shortsightedness. A case in point was extending the growing area into the flatlands beyond the Valpolicella and lowering the parameters regulating the production of Amarone. It was a mistaken move that undermined the relationship between supply and demand by fostering excessive production, which in its turn resulted in a marked drop in quality, prices and image. For consumers it's completely disorienting. How are they to know why one bottle costs twice as much as the other, when both claim to be the same thing? At this point I think the only way out is to insist on the value of recognized brands that are reliable and representative."

Persuasion

The essence of alliance is getting people to act in a mutually beneficial way. Nadia Santini does not look like the sort of person you imagine at the head of a platoon. Smallish in stature, she has an aura of elegant delicacy, with salt-and-pepper hair and a ready smile. Yet she must be endowed with particular gifts of culinary command because she is the chef at the 3 Michelin star Ristorante dal Pescatore at Canneto sull'Oglio, near Mantova. When in 2004 she was awarded the Premio Masi, she spoke about cuisine as the noblest manifestation of generosity and the most tangible symbol of affection. "Above all, cooking is the alchemy of people who work with their hands. It obeys the dictates of ethics and responds to the mystery of taste. Food thus becomes happiness, feeling and an awareness of well-being."

The manner in which Nadia Santini manages to rally the troops and get the very best out of any raw material has more to do with the art of persuasion than with the imposition of authority. It is with vision, patience and gentle coaxing that the humblest ingredients can be transformed into elevated gastronomy.

It may well be that this approach also derives from a typically Venetian attitude to overcoming obstacles. "We like to analyze problems from all possible sides, get to know them through and through, but never attack them head-on. A little gentle cajoling, perhaps, but with intelligence rather than brute strength," says Sandro.

In this sense, he recognizes similar abilities in two other Masi prize winners, though their professional lives have taken diametrically different courses. Novello Finotti is a renowned sculptor who transforms the hardest materials into shapes that embody a silken gentleness and sensuality. He works with bronze, marble and stone, and although his sculpture has changed in idiom over the decades, it rarely fails to exercise a curious magnetism for both eye and hand. "Here's a small, slim man who takes on monoliths and metals, and isn't content until he has made them so pliant that you feel you have to reach out to stroke them. This insistence isn't born of stubbornness, but of deep convictions, and skill in getting around obstacles."

Clearly these are gifts that also underlie the actions of successful diplomats, in the widest sense of the term. One such case in point is Giorgio Zanotto, who was awarded the Masi prize in 1999, shortly before his death. Mayor of Verona from 1956 to 1965, Zanotto continued to play a leading role in a number of institutions that were to have a major positive impact on the economy and culture of the area. "He was a man of great vision, determination and style, unfailingly courteous to a degree that must have been disarming to those who opposed his plans. Verona owes him a great deal, including a powerful, well-structured banking system, the University, the city airport, greatly improved roads, and the development of the trade and agricultural fairs that come under the aegis of Veronafiere. I believe he managed to do so much in various sectors because he foresaw problems that might arise and acted pre-emptively, or found solutions before the obstacle became too complicated. This is precisely how the Most Serene Republic of Venice managed to ensure peace in its territories for such a long time."

Sandro believes that a degree of something akin to diplomacy is also required to make Amarone. The weather can be tricky, and the techniques involved are complex, so producers need to be especially farsighted, determined and adaptable. "In the modern grape-growing world, the climate is mostly hot and dry, and winemakers readily turn to technology to make up for any failing in nature. Here in the Valpolicella, we have to keep and eye on the elements, and our sights on the goal, prepared at all times to juggle with climate, grapes and production methods."

Contemplation of the challenges of making Amarone brings Sandro to a wistful halt. Turning to his bookshelf, he extracts a volume by Giovanni Quintarelli, a Veronese writer of the early 1900s who expressed the essence of the Valpolicella in lyrical terms that still ring true to its twenty-first century inhabitants: "Nature has accomplished something strange and complex for one of its favorite creations," wrote Quintarelli. "Wine, in general, derives from grape juice produced under the heat of the sun in particularly hot countries. Here, on the other hand, at the foot of the Alps, the Mediterranean climate shimmers in the distance. Yet nature seems intent on putting everything it can into producing the most exquisite liquor. Like the swan song that heralds death, so the vine composes its most difficult and beautiful work at the gate to the north, where the cold will deprive it of life. A sort of sunset imbued with magnificent reflections and hues. Creation has invested this wine with wonderful flavors, with delectable tastes, with lovely, fragrant scents. It's a unique delicacy that cannot be analyzed or rated. Who can express perfume, volatility, taste and softness in figures? Works of art are judged the same way, not by measuring or weighing them."

Heritage

Though proud of their past, in general Venetians are too busy focusing on present developments and future aspirations to indulge in nostalgia. This forward-looking attitude has paved the way for widespread prosperity. But it also helps explain the ravages of landscape that industry has brought in its wake. With few exceptions—part of the Valpolicella is one of them—the surroundings of the great Venetian villas have been devoured by voracious modernity with little regard for aesthetics. For anyone who knew and loved the landscape of the Veneto in a past that often failed to provide the wherewithal for survival, it is sometimes difficult to discern recognizable values in contemporary reality. Among the Veneti who have long lived abroad, this has created a form of critical detachment from their origins that can range from discomfort to censure.

One such case is Federico Faggin, whom Sandro describes as a modern version of the Venetian who would set off with his emigrant's suitcase in search of a market that could appreciate what he had to offer. Faggin was born in Vicenza, took a degree in physics in Padua and went on to do such innovative work with the invention of microchips that he soon moved to California, where he founded companies such as ZiLOG, where he conceived and architected the Z80 microprocessor family, and Synaptics, which creates human interface products and technology based on sensory pattern recognition.

When in 1997 Faggin received the Masi prize, he took the opportunity to visit a number of companies in the Vicenza area, and couldn't help comparing two very different approaches to business: that of Silicon Valley, on the one hand, and Vicenza, on the other. Alas, his hometown did not come off very well. He found entrepreneurship in the area to be hampered by a shortage of investment, lack of vision and a devotion to family obligations at the expense of professional excellence. He was particularly shocked to find companies that first and foremost entrusted positions of responsibility to family members, pointing out that this in California would be seen as a form of nepotism.

Clearly, in a sector that is all about innovation, dynamism is interwoven with the introduction of new ideas that accompanies a constant turnover in highly specialized personnel. All that is very un-Venetian. But then, as the Amarone story illustrates, at least part of what the Veneto does well derives from its past, and relies heavily on expertise built up and perfected over several generations.

While Faggin's detachment from his origins borders on rejection, other prominent Veneti living abroad have come to less polarized conclusions. Pietro Cardin, who was born near Treviso, emigrated to France with his family when he was two, and moved to Paris in 1945 to study architecture. He soon found himself designing not buildings but clothes, opening his own fashion house as "Pierre Cardin" in 1950. "When we first contacted him to explain how we wished to honor a fellow countryman with the Premio Masi, he told us he had no interest in being seen as a Venetian," Sandro recalls. "Well, fair enough, that wasn't the image he wished to put across in the early 1990s. Five years later, however, when he had purchased his palazzo in Venice and was spending time there, he called me to ask if the award was still available. I believe that he had recognized some aspects of his own creativity as fitting in with the spirit of Venice, his family having left the Veneto before it became part of his conscious heritage."

Several years after receiving the Masi prize in 1997, Pierre Cardin wrote about Venice as a city "born of the desire for freedom," that offered protection to those suffering persecution and a home to rebel spirits. These elements were essential to the development of the Serenissima, a city-state that demanded government by men of proven ability. In such an atmosphere art and creativity were able to flourish. "I feel at home among this, it gives me joy and inspiration, and I have taken it with me throughout the world. I declare that I am a citizen of Venice."

V

DISCERNING GOALS

I f a winemaker's primary task is to make fine wines, his essential secondary objective must be to promote them: get people to taste them, but also explain them and the land they come from, pointing out what is particular and unique so that wine lovers are able to relate to them with confidence and pleasure. This is an art that requires skill, foresight and courage. Not long ago, Canadian wine writer David Lawrason described Sandro Boscaini as "a man smitten by wine—in particular the Veronese wines of his homeland in north eastern Italy . . . He is also inquiring, restless, worldly and very intelligent—all of which has led him to one innovation after another, and a great ability to educate and inspire and promote."[1]

The outstanding stature that Masi enjoys at home and abroad is the fruit of these gifts, and the determination to put "quality before quantity, propriety before profit, modesty before self-assertion and loyalty before immediate advantage," to borrow the words of another perspicacious wine writer.[2] The winery's goals involve at least three interrelated spheres: the local dimension, meaning the heritage and image of the Valpolicella; the wider picture of the legacy of Venice and its values; and the

---

1 In the pleasant, informative wine website www.winealign.com, November 3, 2009

2 Nicolas Belfrage, *Life Beyond Lambrusco*, Sidgwick & Jackson, London, 1985, p. 193

potential of the appassimento technique much further afield, in distant countries and continents.

As far as the Valpolicella is concerned, there are three aspects that Sandro has taken on board. The first involves preserving the integrity of the area, which in its turn implies promoting quality viticulture and persuading oenophiles, and in general those who appreciate the value of good, locally grown food, to include the Valpolicella among their prime destinations in Italy. Though this may sound like an echo of the Slow Food movement, it actually anticipated what that organization originally set out to do by several years. In the early 1970s, Sandro's business expertise got him involved, initially as a consultant and later as managing director, with the Istituto Enologico Italiano. The main focus of this institution was the promotion and sales of fine Italian wines, an objective it had hitherto pursued quite effectively, but with a certain insouciance for paperwork. While Sandro was sorting through the records and putting things to rights, he observed the Istituto's close ties with the Mondadori publishing house in Milan. One of Mondadori's most prominent authors was Mario Soldati, whose articles for popular magazines such as *Grazia* and *Epoca* alerted the reading public to the existence of Italy's unique wines, foods and landscapes. "Soldati wasn't a wine specialist, but he was a great writer with a wonderful eye for detail," Sandro recalls. "His chatty, slightly quirky book *Vino al vino*[3] is really a series of portraits of people and the wines they make, so vivid that you can practically taste the wine through the words. I began to realize that people are happy to experience new wines and landscapes if they are introduced to them the right way."

Encouraging winelovers to visit the Valpolicella obviously meant providing them with somewhere attractive to stay. One of the fruits of Masi's collaboration with the Serego Alighieri family has been the transformation of part of the farm buildings on the historic estate into a spacious guesthouse. Moreover,

---

3 Mario Soldati, *Vino al vino—alla ricerca del vino genuino*, Mondadori, Milan 1981.

much of the handsome breakfast served there comes from a farsighted approach to estate produce: Serego Alighieri jams and honey of such excellence that anyone who tastes them will need no further encouragement to visit the estate wine shop, where they can also stock up on extra virgin olive oil, balsamic vinegar and the Vialone Nano rice that bear the same patrician label.

This is not a question of simply jumping on the artisan foods bandwagon. "Most people know about the balsamic vinegar of Modena," Sandro explains, "but few realize that many areas of Italy renowned for the production of good red wines also have a tradition for cooked and reduced wines, as well as aromatic vinegars. They were used as special condiments for both sweet and savory dishes, and for preserving. In the Serego Alighieri archives we actually found a recipe for what today would be considered a balsamic vinegar, so we went to one of the best artisan vinegar producers in Modena to have it made up, using musts from the Serego Alighieri estates. This product is directly related to Amarone, because it is made with the juice from semi-dried grapes that has been reduced and then blended with vinegar obtained from Valpolicella wine. The result is an exceptional product. By the same token we also wished to draw attention to the fact that the family used to possess a substantial tract of land south of Verona, around Isola della Scala, where there was an age-old tradition of rice cultivation: maps in the vast family archive describe this tract of land as *'risare Serego Alighieri.'* The area is flat, with plenty of spring water channeled to feed the rice fields, which produce a rare variety, the Vialone nano, which is ideal for risotto. It seemed logical to recover that tradition, not least because a good risotto pairs so well with our wines."

The second aspect regarding the Valpolicella is an effort to redress a number of serious problems that have come in the wake of Amarone's recent success. When the Valpolicella D.O.C. was first introduced in 1968, there were few producers of Amarone, all of them traditional wineries like the Boscaini concern located in the hilly areas that are uniquely well suited to grapegrowing. Viticulture was also widespread to the east, however, in the Valpantena and beyond, where soils and climate are different, and in the flatter lands to the south, towards Pescantina and Parona, where the climate is less favorable for grape growing. Since these were not prime growing areas, the farmers largely sold their grapes to big cooperative wineries that produced low-end wines for chains and supermarkets. Because the cooperative wineries represented a large number of growers, however, they wielded a certain political clout, and at the time managed to ensure that the contours of the Valpolicella growing area were drawn with a wide enough sweep to include them. At the time, doubts were expressed, though to little avail, about the wisdom of a single category that comprised both the traditional Valpolicella winemakers and growers from areas that were in many respects different. The term *Classico* was introduced to differentiate the former from the latter, but this was hardly self-explanatory to most consumers, not least because nothing was done officially to clarify the matter. Sandro was so upset about this lack of vision that he actually resigned from the Consortium. Some fifteen years later, wine growers in the wider area began to realize that Amarone had become a name of such gratifying prestige that they could cash in on its fame with their own version of the wine. Granted, the grapes weren't as good and didn't naturally dry out well in such locations, where there was no time-honored practice of appassimento anyway. But technology stepped in to lend a hand, and the local Consortium of Wine Producers did not have the foresight to act preventively. The ensuing damage was inevitable.

"I have nothing against advanced technology as such," says Sandro. "Far from it. We at Masi were actually among the first wineries to take a serious look at what modern grape-drying technology could do to help appassimento in difficult years, when the climate was bad. But this is quite different to creating a totally artificial environment in which appassimento is forced upon the grapes. By exploiting these techniques, bottles of what, according to the book, could be called Amarone were released early on the market at much lower prices, precisely because they sidestepped the long, drawn-out traditional methods that have made the acclaimed wine so rare and special. When wine labeled as Amarone started to appear in supermarkets, the immediate commercial return was inevitably overshadowed by the long-term damage to substance and image, a fact most of the new entries were unable to grasp."

The results of such benighted policies have been predictably depressing. The 6.75 million liters of Amarone that were sold in 2008 had grown to 9 million by 2009. In terms of bottles, this meant a surge from nine to twelve million in the space of just two vintages, 2006 and 2007. For all this increase in volume, however, the value of sales dropped by sixteen percent from a total of 81 million Euros to 68 million. By the same token, between 2007 and 2009, the wholesale price of Amarone per liter dropped from around 12 Euros to 7.50. The price paid for grapes also diminished, while the costs of production actually rose. Granted, the economic crisis was already affecting markets, but this only aggravated what was already a problematic situation. To add insult to injury, when Amarone received the coveted D.O.C.G. status in 2010, no efforts were made to restrict the growing area to the Valpolicella hillsides. The only consolation was the reduction of the percentage of grapes used for making Amarone in any given vineyard from an excessive 70% to 60%.

Such schizophrenic commercial behavior has been hard on quality producers and extremely confusing for the consumer, especially wine lovers approaching Amarone for the first time. They would have read about the wine, heard about its stature, imagined its velvety gentleness, then found bottles at less than half the expected price on supermarket shelves. It didn't taste that memorable, so was Amarone overrated, or was this not the real thing? This state of ambiguity didn't actually affect Masi that much, since the winery had such a widely established name and continued to net awards the world over. Yet it did have negative connotations for the Valpolicella, suggesting that winemakers cared little for quality. Sandro realized that only collective effort could straighten the picture, so he went round to talk with the other historic producers, suggesting that together they could and should take a stand.

Apart from turning competitors into colleagues, at least to some extent, the outcome of these discussions was the foundation in 2009 of an association of winemakers called the Famiglie dell'Amarone d'Arte, who all share certain traits: they are family concerns that have been making the wine for at least fifteen years; they are all grape growers as well as winemakers; each produces at least 20,000 bottles of Amarone a year; each exports to five or more foreign markets; they wait until at least thirty months from the vintage to release their Amarone, which have an alcohol content of not less than 15 percent; and they agree to release no Amarone in bad years. In other words, they are wineries of proven devotion to quality.

With Sandro as their captain and helmsman, within a year the members of the association had grown to twelve: Allegrini, Begali, Brigaldara, Masi Agricola, Musella, Nicolis, Speri, Tedeschi, Tenuta Sant'Antonio, Tommasi, Venturini and Zenato, who together accounted for nearly 577 hectares of vineyard in the best growing areas dedicated to the production of Amarone, with an overall output of two million bottles in 2009, totaling a value of 29 million Euros, when there were still only ten members.

By September 2010, the association was ready to publish a manifesto describing the characteristics of Amarone d'Arte, and pointing out how the image and essence of Amarone were threatened by excessive production and a drop in quality and prices. In this declaration, there is a paragraph that resounds with Sandro's voice: "Amarone d'Arte is an ambassador of 'Made in Italy' in the world, as its individuality is recognized in its high quality and unique characteristics. Amarone Families are the guardians of tradition for this great wine, exploiting invaluable experience reaped over years of producing Amarone. They influence the success of Amarone on international markets with their commitment to quality and innovation."[4]

---

4 *Manifesto delle Famiglie dell'Amarone d'Arte*, presented in Milan, 14 September 2010.

As proof that this was no idle talk, the Amarone Families pledged to adhere to stringent parameters that would "ensure the noble characteristics of the product." They also opted to distinguish their bottles of Amarone with a small round hologram featuring a central 'A' cradled by the name of the association and topped with symmetrical tendrils: a simple emblem, but one that would be immediately recognizable to consumers. Next came a series of tasting events aimed at further acquainting established and promising markets with the depth and complexity of the wine. The first took place in Verona, Rome and Milan. Next came an important presentation in London in 2009, followed by participation at the Decanter Fine Wine Encounter. Towards the end of 2010, a major tasting event was held in Zurich, underlining Switzerland's historic importance as a market for Amarone. Not only do the Swiss prefer wine to beer, but they are such discerning drinkers as to position their country second only to Canada as Amarone's most important market. Hardly surprisingly, early in October that same year the Amarone Families staged a similar encounter in Toronto, followed by one in New York. Redress is under way, and will no doubt lead to other innovative projects and benefits.

One of these is already taking shape. It concerns the group's collective effort to save the Bottega del Vino in Verona, which had been going through difficult times on account of disagreements among the previous management. By taking a direct role in the future of this historic establishment, the Famiglie dell'Amarone d'Arte are not only saving a high temple of wine. They are also ensuring that Verona maintains its role as the wine capital, and that the Bottega del Vino continues to soldier on as the "great tavern of the people," as the German writer Hans Barth has so aptly described it.

The third project originating in the Valpolicella revolves around Recioto, once Verona's most famous product. Like sweet wines in general, today the deep red *Vinum Reticum* praised by Pliny the Elder is at pains to establish a niche for itself on domestic and foreign markets. It's as though societies surrounded by sugary processed foods are no longer attuned to what is subtly sweet, with gentle, lingering tannins and a clean finish. Arguably some of the problem lies in the perception that Recioto is a dessert wine, firstly because consumers tend to think of dessert wines as being white, golden or a light, pinky apricot color, and secondly because by and large people prefer to devote their intake of alcohol to the dry wines that accompany the main courses of a meal. Granted, there are exceptions, such as Sauternes and Canada's Icewine, which is why Sandro has been talking with Donald Ziraldo, a fellow Venetian who is famed for having introduced Icewine production to Canada. Together they are working on a Recioto that is lighter in hue, with plenty of fruit but less tannic.

"Recioto is like a slice of history that is looking for its place in the present," says Sandro. "It's unique, both rural and patrician, a wine to love, to rediscover, perhaps to recreate and certainly to launch anew." This is an opinion shared by Severino Barzan, the historic host of the Bottega del Vino in Verona, a man with a remarkable understanding of how young wines will evolve and what the market is ready to understand and enjoy. Barzan's nose and palate for wine futures has led him to buy *en primeur*, both in Italy and in France, so that his cellar is now one of the country's finest. At present he is a firm believer in the intrinsic beauty and future potential of Recioto, but he admits that there is work to be done so that wine lovers know what to expect and how to appreciate it. "When you run a wine shop like the Bottega you have to be an educator," he declares. "We provide the right glass for a given wine, and always rinse it with wine before pouring to enhance the impact of the aromas. When customers are used to this they wouldn't dream of tasting a wine without it. They become demanding, and that for me is stimulating. It spurs me on to learn something every day as well. There are some very interesting wines that are underestimated because people simply don't know enough about them. The foremost is Recioto, which can be one of the greatest red wines in the world. But there are some revolting concoctions out there that also call themselves Recioto. Customers sometimes ask me which is the true Recioto, and whether the sparkling version is the real thing. You can tell them that fizzy Recioto is an abomination, but it's difficult to give them an account of how the wine should be without going into too much detail. What we really need is someone ready to devote time and effort into establishing the proper parameters of Recioto, so that anything else has to go by another name. I would be happy to support a project of this sort, not least by pairing Recioto with certain cheeses rather than desserts."

Masi seems to be ready to pick up the gauntlet, having realized over the decades that certain vineyards are particularly well suited to producing grapes for Recioto, while others lend themselves better to Amarone. Apart from identifying historic *crus* for Recioto, the winery has also opted for a slightly different approach to drying. A greater degree of *Botrytis* is desirable for Recioto, and this comes about naturally at an altitude of around 200 meters, for example in the vineyards around Gargagnago, rather than higher up the hillside, where a cooler, breezier climate impedes the development of molds.

Forty years ago, around eighty percent of the grapes selected for drying would have been used for making the sweet wine. Today the ratio has been reduced to about five percent. Yet the venerable Veronese custom of offering honored guests a glass of Recioto has survived, which must hearten quality winemakers set on familiarizing the wider commercial market with such a unique product.

Masi produces three distinctive Reciotos that offer an enticing taste of the range, subtlety and refinement of the genre. The Casal Dei Ronchi Recioto Classico made at the Serego Alighieri estate is a deep, dark, almost viscous red that is initially quite sweet in the mouth, with aromas of cherries in spirit and walnuts followed by a touch of plum-like acidity and an elegantly tannic finish. The Masi Amabile degli Angeli Recioto Classico is also a deep, dark red, cherry sweet on the nose, but with a delectable balance of sweetness and acidity in the mouth that make it particularly easy to drink. Both of these wines will lose some of their initial sweetness after five years or so of aging, acquiring mature, spicy notes slightly reminiscent of port.

The Masi Mezzanella Amandorlato Recioto, on the other hand, is a rarity that explains the relationship between Recioto and Amarone. Fermentation is protracted for longer, so that the wine naturally tends towards semi-dry. As the name suggests, it is almond sweet on the nose and initially in the mouth, after which it gives way to plenty of ripe fruit and a finish that is unexpectedly dry and clean. In fact it has a total acidity that is slightly higher than the other two Reciotos, with half the amount of residual sugar.

These three magnificent products are like thoroughbred horses carefully tended in a stable and occasionally taken out to the paddock to stretch their legs. When they first appear at the grand racetrack they will be considered interesting outsiders. Once people have witnessed their performance, however, they will become stars, with all the media coverage they deserve.

Horizons

The Masi alliance with the Serego Alighieri estate dates back a long time, to when Count Pieralvise's father used to sell his grapes to Sandro's father, calling upon him occasionally for advice and ultimately agreeing to the sale of the building and farmhouses that have become the Masi headquarters in Gargagnago. But there is more to the story than this. Their collaboration has been a model for farsighted partnership that has paved the way for further Masi projects.

One of the most recent has been the purchase of land eminently suitable for viticulture in southern Tuscany, in the Montecucco D.O.C. growing area, which is in many respects similar to that of neighboring Montalcino. Though the new plantings at Poderi del Bello Ovile and the actual winemaking are handled by Masi, it's a Serego Alighieri project that relates to the family's desire to recover its Tuscan origins. Indeed, the name of the estate is a quotation from Dante's *Paradiso*.[5] There is more to this than astute marketing, however. The Masi techni-

---

5 Dante Alighieri, *Paradiso*, canto xxv, 5

cal team has identified an area particularly well suited to traditional Tuscan varieties such as Sangiovese, Canaiolo, Colorino and Ciliegiolo. The first fruit of the new enterprise is the Poderi del Bello Ovile I.G.T. red wine, a Sangiovese, Canaiolo and Ciliegiolo blend that is full-bodied, complex and elegant, yet versatile enough to accompany both red and white meats.

Another interesting venture is Masi's collaboration with the Bossi Fedrigotti winery near Rovereto, in the Trentino region, a short journey north from the Valpolicella along the Adige Valley. Like the Serego Alighieri family, the Bossi Fedrigottis had been farming their estates for many centuries, though they had "only" been making wine there for around three hundred years. In fact their first vintage, harvested in 1697, is one of the earliest recorded in Italy. Count Federico Bossi Fedrigotti, father of the current owners, substantially reformed how their land was farmed in the mid twentieth century, introducing a degree of modernization that kept them abreast of the market. It was he, for example, who created the first Bordeaux blend in Italy, back in 1961: Fojaneghe, an enticing and extremely successful marriage of Merlot and Cabernet grown on wide basalt-rich terraces overlooking the Adige River. When the property passed on to his offspring, there was no one living full time at the estate, and though each of the three of them put what they could into the winery, it inevitably lost its focus, not least because it was producing around fifteen different wines. Aware of the mutual benefits of the Serego Alighieri-Masi relationship, the Bossi Fedrigottis decided to seek a similar partnership. Isabella, who was a Masi prize winner in 1995 and an old friend of Sandro's, agreed to ask Sandro for advice. He saw the opening as an excellent opportunity for both parties. "From our point of view, the estate had all the characteristics we are interested in supporting and developing," Sandro explains. "It was part of the larger area that came under Venetian influence, it was an estate with an important name and history, the vineyards were in excellent locations, and the Bossi Fedrigottis, who wanted to remain involved in the future of their property, already had working cellars that only required a little updating."

They started to collaborate in 2007, with Masi providing technical support and its international sales network to help the Bossi Fedrigotti wines establish themselves on markets at home and abroad. One of the first things the Masi Technical Team insisted on was the reduction of the wines to five, with an accent on local varietals. Alongside the original Fojaneghe blend, these consisted of a fine Pinot Grigio, a well-structured, aromatic Gewürztraminer, the delightful light red Marzemino, and the full-bodied Teroldego red. Dante Cavazzani, senior Masi cellarman and a Trentino by birth, agreed to return to his homeland and oversee updating the cellars and the winemaking and aging processes. This included improved temperature control and better use of barriques. It also meant more selective work in the vineyard, especially with the whites, where staggered harvesting could ensure a better balance of aromas and acidity.

Located in three different areas, the 40 hectares of Bossi Fedrigotti vineyards now follow the protocol for premium grape production established by the Masi Technical Group. Fortnightly bulletins are sent out to the vineyard managers with instructions on what needs to be done when and where. This rationalization of all stages leading up to the harvest also contributes to optimization in the cellar, from fermentation through to aging. The overall outcome has been a marked increase in quality and greater commercial visibility, while remaining true to the winery's historic image.

In its pursuit of excellence in the wider area that once came under the aegis of Venice, Masi has also invested in Friuli, marrying local grape varieties with the Valpolicella appassimento technique to persuasive effect. Twenty years ago Sandro was already eyeing the prime grape growing areas of Friuli to locate exactly what he had in mind. A wide stretch of land gently sloping down towards the sea at Castions di Strada, to the southeast of the region, seemed to answer all his requirements. The sedimentary soils consisted of loose clay with a gravelly substratum and sufficient underground water for viticulture. Moreover, the proximity of the sea would have beneficial effects on the climate, making it temperate, dry and well-ventilated.

"We ended up by planting over 200 hectares of vineyard at the Tenuta Stra del Milione estate. I had a vision of producing two different types of wine there. On the one hand, what you might call 'entry products,' but very good ones that would stand out for their excellent price-quality ratio. They are based on native varieties such as the red Refosco and Raboso grapes, and the whites Pinot Grigio and Pinot Bianco. We produce a fresh, fruity and approachable red wine, a rosé and a surprisingly elegant, substantial white, which we have simply called 'Modello delle Venezie.' These are not meant to be high-end wine shop products, but extremely presentable house wines for restaurants and hotels. At the other end of the spectrum we also produce what we think of as a 'Supervenetian,' by which I mean an original, cutting edge interpretation of the Venetian viticultural heritage. The Masianco white is made with two indigenous varieties: late-harvested Verduzzo, which provides smoothness, body and richness, and Pinot Grigio, which accounts for the elegant nose and attractive fruitiness. The other important wine from the Friuli estate is Grandarella, which is made with partially dried Refosco and Carmenère. The technique is similar to that of Amarone, with appassimento for around fifty days, which contributes great concentration and complexity, and aging in oak casks for twenty-four months. This is a curious case of innovation. What is new isn't so much the blend or the technique, but the combination of the two. The outcome is a majestic wine that combines strength and great elegance."

The Friuli estate doesn't have its own cellars, so initially the wines were made at a third party winery in the area. Later, vinification, aging and bottling were moved to the Valgatara facility. The arrangement works well thanks to Masi's considerable experience in handling logistics, a sector now directed by Sandro's brother Bruno, an engineer whose return to the family firm has introduced great expertise in supplies, bottling and shipment.

Masi's involvement in different types of venture beyond the Valpolicella is likely to expand. Sandro admits that his aim is to have a stake in all the main wine genres of the Veneto, including the production of Prosecco. In fact he is currently looking into the possibility of taking over or working with a property in the Conegliano district. The Boscainis have well-established ties with the area, Sandro's brother Sergio having studied at the Conegliano Institute of Viticulture. To add to which, Andrea Dal Cin, Masi's much-traveled enologist, is originally from Conegliano. This, along with Sandro's proven foresight and determination, suggests that the project is likely to become a reality in the near future.

New worlds

Masi is a company with a thoroughly Venetian countenance, and an international profile. Sandro has always kept the wider world in mind, not only in terms of the markets that could absorb his wine, but also as a way of discovering new elements that might fit in with his Venetian values project. In the early 1980s, it was the Masi aptitude for outreach that brought Daniel Block from Seattle to Italy, where he became Sandro's right-hand man for marketing and business. Since then, the entire company management has grown increasingly international, with a marked preference for local experts as directors of Masi operations abroad. Indeed, today there are seven non-Italian heads of export, which accounts for 90% of the winery's sales.

Hardly surprisingly, it is Amarone and Campofiorin that take pride of place on foreign markets. Because both of these wines are as much the fruit of particular techniques as they are of native grape varieties, it occurred to Sandro that the winery might equally export its expertise in appassimento. The New World seemed a particularly attractive proposition, largely because growers are free to plant what they want where they like, without the constraints in terms of variety and quantity that prevail in European viticulture.

Though Sandro travels a great deal, he knows that he can count on a well-assorted team of highly professional collaborators at home. They include Lidia Corso, who is overall head of administration, Omero Gobbo, in charge of all the winegrowing estates, and Giovanni Girelli, who handles purchases and maintenance. The outcome is a form of team spirit that allows those who administrate the company to feel they are in contact with both the wine technicians, directed by Andrea Dal Cin, and with the logistics sector headed by Bruno Boscaini. Interwoven with all these activities is Canadian-born Luc Desroches, the Masi business manager, and Alessandra, Sandro's daughter, who manages sales administration with admirable efficiency.

"We devoted many years to researching the winegrowing areas of the New World, to see what would suit us best, and what was best suited to the grape varieties and the techniques we could introduce. New Zealand was one of the most enticing contenders. But we decided in the end that the enormous distance and the frequency of problematic weather conditions made it too difficult to manage. Australia was another possibility, but here again the distance is daunting. Moreover, Australia has created a certain image for its wines, which cater to a vast market and are distinctly standardized, so that consumers expect them to be just as they were last time they tasted them. This all seemed to be at odds with what we had in mind. We finally found a satisfactory situation at Tupungato, in the Mendoza region of Argentina, thanks to Lanfranco Paronetto's excellent advice. The added boon was that many of the farmers who had settled in the area originally came from the Veneto and had preserved much of their original culture and language. So our new project was in various respects a further pursuit of Venetian values."

The 160-hectare Arboleda estate is located at an altitude of 3,444 feet (1,050 meters), on a gently sloping plateau backed by the snow-capped Andean Cordillera range, about 620 miles (1,000 km) from Buenos Aires. The soils are loose, with plenty of organic matter, and the semi-desert climate features average summer temperatures of 72° F (22° C), and winters a little above freezing. During the season when the grapes are growing and maturing, there is a substantial drop in night temperatures, a feature that contributes to the quality of the harvest. Average annual rainfall is about 7.8 inches (200 mm), which is less than a quarter that of the Valpolicella. Because the atmosphere is excessively dry, the Masi team decided to introduce an artificial lake and an irrigation system that would add the required degree of humidity, making the microclimate better suited to the Veronese grape varieties that were introduced: Corvina and Pinot Grigio to blend with the Argentinean Malbec and Torrontés also grown on the estate, plus a small experimental vineyard in which other Italian varieties such as Rondinella, Croatina, Nero d'Avola, Primitivo di Gioia and Ancelotta were put to the test.

In their new home, ripe Corvina grapes achieve a higher concentration of sugars than they do in the Valpolicella, with deeper color and naturally soft tannins. To date, the 120 hectares of productive vineyards produce three remarkable wines, which all combine a certain Argentinean generosity and exuberance with the elegance and approachability of wines from the Veneto. The secret of these happy unions is the introduction for the red grapes of appassimento, duly adapted to the new environment. For the Corbec red, a 70/30% blend of Corvina and Malbec grapes, drying takes place on trays placed in a well-ventilated shed. The floor is constantly watered to increase the ambient humidity, and within the space of a mere 15-20 days, the grapes lose around 20% of their weight, which is judged to be ideal for what the Masi team has in mind. Corbec is unique among Argentinean wines, with an impressive bouquet of extra-ripe cherries, a full, fruity body and an almost virile, tannic finish. Passo Doble, the second Tupungato red, is made with 70% Malbec grapes that undergo a second fermentation with 30% semi-dried Corvina. On the nose and in the mouth the cherry notes typical of Corvina soften the more overt spice and plum flavors associated with Malbec, creating a wine that is full of youthful vigor, but not wanting in finesse. Its sibling is Passo Blanco, in which the elegance of Pinot Grigio is married with Torrontés, a widely planted aromatic Argentinean variety. The outcome is a white wine with a distinctly aromatic nose, followed by plenty of grapefruit, lime and minerals in the mouth.

The overall effect is full-bodied, yet pleasantly fresh and elegant as well.

Masi is currently also looking into the possibility of lending its viticultural expertise to another South American country, Brazil. Like Argentina, from the second half of the nineteenth century Brazil attracted thousands of Venetian immigrants, who largely preserved their original language and culture once they had settled there. Many of them ended up farming land where they cultivated grapes for nondescript commercial wines, while tending small vineyards for their own use planted with the cuttings they had brought over with them many years before. A friend of Sandro's named Don Ivo Pasa, a Catholic priest born in Brazil to a family originally from the Veneto, contacted Masi to see if the winery's experience could not be put to good use among his flock in the Rio Grande do Sur area. The idea was to help farmers improve their plantings, select their grapes, and make quality wines, which would give them some profile and better returns.

It is characteristic of Sandro that he was prepared to look into the project even if it was of no particular immediate benefit for Masi. "Brazil is not renowned for its wines, but I thought it would be interesting to see what they were doing there. When we discovered that many of the grape growers were actually familiar with Veronese varieties and techniques even though they weren't using them for their commercial products, it was hard not to get involved. We haven't signed and sealed anything formally, but I think something may yet come out of this curious encounter."

Sandro's eye for promising markets and potential wine-growing areas has led him to set off with Lanfranco Paronetto and Andrea Dal Cin to visit various countries in Eastern Europe and beyond, from Romania to Georgia. Not all of them have related to viticultural investment as such. Indeed, at the 2010 edition of the Premio Masi, the award for Wine Civilization went to the Eastern Orthodox Archbishop Sergi Chekurishvili of Nekresi, who has done so much to rescue his country's ancient winegrowing traditions from the slump that followed the Russian embargo on Georgian wines. "Georgia is thought to be the birthplace of winemaking," Sandro explains. "When the Russian market that absorbed 80% of the country's wine was suddenly closed, the entire historic heritage risked collapse, along with the lives of the farmers and winemakers involved. In the space of a few years, Archibishop Sergi has helped redress the situation, promoting his country's wines and welcoming the International Organization for Vine and Wine's annual conference there in 2010. This is an admirable accomplishment for which we should all be grateful."

One of Masi's most recent and unexpected destinations is India. Sandro's son Raffaele, who heads the Technical team, visited Bangalore in July 2010 with enologist Andrea del Cin at the invitation of an Indian business conglomerate interested in branching into wine production. "The core interests of the group range from steel to plant nurseries," Raffaele recounts, "but they also produce beer and spirits. Back in 1985 they bought a paper mill outside Bangalore, which they closed ten years later, with the idea that the land could be used for growing grapes. They called us in as consultants. The location is about 2,900 feet (900 meters) above sea level, backed by mountains and with a plentiful supply of water. I was amazed to discover that there are well-tended vineyards in the area, with poles made of stone rather than wood. The market for wine in India is still small, but it's growing, and for the moment is largely fed by Indian wines, some of which leave much to be desired. Quality wines imported from abroad are fantastically expensive, so well-made Indian wines are very successful on the domestic market, and this is something we would like to get involved in.

"The Masi Technical Group feels that their initial in-volvement would probably revolve around experimenting with appassimento, to give Indian wines greater complexity and individuality. The Indian project is still in its infancy, and will require time to develop. You can select from what nature has to offer, but you can't speed up the growing process."

While Masi's involvement in winemaking outside the Veneto, and indeed outside Italy, is the fruit of a deliberate policy, the winery's products have also helped shape wines made by other growers in distant countries. This indirect influence is largely attributable to the fame of Amarone, and to the remarkable impact of Campofiorin, the appassimento technique and double fermentation.

There are currently wineries in countries as different as New Zealand, Chile, Australia, Canada and the USA that are using appassimento to give their wines greater individuality. "The person who started this trend a good quarter of a century ago was Joseph Grilli at his winery near Adelaide," Sandro points out. "He visited us several times, and we had some long chats together with Nino Franceschetti. He was a very bright young man, full of curiosity. A few years later he brought us some bottles of what he had made. They were fantastic wines, some of the best in Australia according to various critics. I paid him all due compliments, but pointed out that I didn't think the word 'Amarone' should feature on the label. It didn't come from the Valpolicella, or from the classic grapes, so it couldn't claim to belong to our historic tradition. His wine was something different, and that's how it should be promoted. In the end he called it Joseph, like his own name, explaining on the back label that it was made in the Amarone style."

Gino Cuneo in the Pacific Northwest of the United States partially dries Sangiovese and Nebbiolo for his Seccopassa red, adopting "the same winemaking process that is used to make the world famous Venetian Amarone wines... Following the Venetian tradition, the clusters are first individually laid out on drying racks, and then dried under controlled temperature and humidity for three-and-a-half to four months resulting in a 30% to 35% weight loss." Another case in point is the Hobbs winery in Australia's Barossa Valley, which produces a "full-bodied Australian Amarone-style Shiraz," made by "blending traditional drying methods with our own style." Or indeed the various Niagara wineries in Canada that are all taking a lead from the time-honored Valpolicella tradition.

According to a Latin proverb, emulation is the whetstone of talent. It is also the highest form of flattery, and not without risks. These seem to loom too close for comfort when an on-line forum that claims to be "the largest winemaking and grape growing discussion (. . .) completely devoted to sharing a wealth of information and learning the ins and outs of (. . .) wine" publishes a comment in which the author declares that he is "thinking of getting some plastic bread racks from a grocery store and drying in my garage, with a fan blasting them (the grapes) at all times and a dehumidifier at the ready."[6]

Sandro often laments the appearance of an "Amarone without history" in his native Valpolicella, or rather in the extended growing area little suited to the production of such a special wine. He would no doubt equally regret most "Amarone-style" wines made without history. "Appassimento isn't a magic wand that can turn something very average into something memorable," he declares. "It's a technique that has a reason to be in a given area, where it has had over 2,000 years to develop. And it may also help elsewhere, but only after the necessary in-depth analysis of existing conditions and the desired outcome. It's not that I'm afraid of competition, because I know perfectly well that the Amarone growing area and the wines made there are totally unique. But I am concerned about winemakers who take short cuts to acquire visibility."

Back at the Valgatara winery, the Masi technical team occasionally gathers together for a blind tasting of New World wines made with semi-dried grapes, which usually include at least one of their own. Each is graded according to color, bouquet, taste, finish and the overall balance of these elements, and when the labels are revealed there is rarely a product that scores anywhere near either of the Masi wines. This is not a question of recognizing their own house style and congratulating themselves for their achievement. It has more to do with knowing how to fashion wines, rather than follow wine fashions.

When Sandro wishes to explain his approach to the art and craft of making wine, he sometimes resorts to the words of Frenchman Émile Peynaud, recipient of the Masi Civiltà del

---

6 See www.winepress.us

Vino award in 1989 and arguably the greatest wine technician and philosopher of the twentieth century. "In the end, what's important for us wine men is that the civilization of wine should continue. Wine, today just as yesterday and tomorrow, continues to embody a double communion with nature (by means of the vegetal mystery and the miracle of fermentation) and with man, who wants to make it and devotes all his knowledge, labor, patience, care and love to doing so. Because there is no valid outcome without love."

VI

CONVIVIALITY

In the classical Greek world, wine was part of the ritual that accompanied the *symposium*, where like-minded people met up to discuss politics, philosophy, military valor, love and ethics. The ritual part imposed moderation in the quantity of wine imbibed, and thus in the opinions expressed. The word *symposium* itself, which sounds rather serious to modern ears, actually means fellow-drinker. As for the ancient Romans, they drank their wines at banquets, which they called *convivial*; the word derives from the union of *com*, meaning "together," and *vivere*, "to live." Here again, it suggests an occasion that mixes sociability with knowledge and pleasure.

This is an approach that fits Amarone perfectly. Getting to know Amarone means living with the wine and appreciating its individuality, watching it evolve and enjoying its company. It's a conversational sort of wine for sharing with friends, for sipping rather than gulping down, for a quiet gathering rather than a wild party.

Sandro Boscaini describes Amarone as *suadente*; the Italian word means persuasive, conciliatory and slightly flattering. It suggests the way Amarone gratifies the drinker, not only because it is rounded, subtle and inviting, but also because it expresses a positive image of the world in general. The most sensual of wines, Amarone also engages the mind, which is why it enhances the sensation of well-being.

"One thing I always notice when taking part in a tasting of different Amarones is the way the initial hush, almost ecclesiastical in reverence, gives way to a happy hum of conversation, a sort of healthy euphoria that soon replaces the clinical coldness typical of tasting sessions," says Sandro. "It's as though the exuberance of the wine itself were contagious—and perhaps it is, because an aura of friendliness always seems to permeate the event."

What this final chapter hopes to do is offer hints on how to select an Amarone, and the best way to store, serve and savor it. The section is intended as a small, informal guided tour to the remarkable universe of taste, put together with the help of eight experts in matching wine with food. To use Sandro's slightly tongue-in-cheek epithet, four of them speak in dialect, while the others are more cosmopolitan in idiom. They start with a local couple whose busy professional lives do not stop them from cooking and drinking well, often with guests. Next come two Veronese purveyors of gourmet products, and the manager of a historic wine shop and restaurant in Verona. Finally there are two restaurateurs of international acclaim, a well-known personality who has also proved himself to be an original food writer, and a sommelier with the vision and experience to reconcile east with west.

Buying

Choosing an Amarone is a question of taste. The twelve members of the Famiglie dell'Amarone d'Arte association of premium producers already encompass a wide range of wines that speak for different soils, microclimates, conditions for appassimento, duration of aging, and so on. Masi itself makes five Amarones, which share family traits but embody different styles. Taste, of course, is both a subjective and an objective phenomenon. Over and above the question of personal predilection, there is also the matter of how the wine marries with food, and how it will age, since the aging potential and the maturation curve also vary in relation to the style.

Some people enjoy the more rounded, full-bodied kind of Amarone that fills the palate with intense aromas of ripe fruit: the Costasera Amarone, for instance, with its wealth of cooked cherry and hints of cacao and cinnamon. Others prefer a certain austerity, with greater emphasis on tannic structure, which suggests that the Mazzano Amarone might be more to their liking.

These are subtle differences that make for an interesting comparison, but shouldn't lead to exclusion. At all events, once the personal preference has been established, there are other essential factors to take into account: vintage, and whether or not the wine is intended for immediate consumption. Though Masi's Amarones are already enjoyable to drink three or four years after harvest, their potential for aging is magnificent. These are wines whose structure will continue to evolve for at least ten years after harvest, along with the powerful aromas of ripe fruit and a certain youthful exuberance. The wine then begins to lose some of its original fruity character, but instead gains hints of aromatic herbs that contribute to refinement and elegance. Rich, spicy perfumes prevail on the nose, and in the mouth the wine is intense, elegant and velvety, with smooth tannins and a long finish. "A good vintage will age for a good thirty-five to forty years," Sandro points out, "and an average one for around twenty."

Three of the Masi Amarones are the product of single vineyards that invest the wine with particular features. Campolongo di Torbe comes from a high-lying vineyard on the west side of the Marano Valley, where soils rich in Eocene limestone and basalt give the wine its characteristic hint of bitter almond and cherrystone.

The second *cru* is the Mazzano Amarone, which comes from a deeply sloping vineyard on the opposite side of the Marano Valley. Because this is one of the highest vineyards in the Valpolicella, the prevailing atmospheric conditions are perfect for *in loco serego*. The resulting wine has great depth and structure, marrying slightly austere nobility with gentle tannins and velvety elegance.

Vaio Armaron Serego Alighieri, Masi's third *cru*, is made from grapes grown and dried on the Serego Alighieri estate, one of the most prestigious cru sites of the Valpolicella Classica, located between 180 and 265 meters (590–870 feet) above sea level. It is Masi's most traditional Amarone, with a complex bouquet and notes of overripe cherry and cooked plums that reveal its kinship to Recioto.

For the Costasera Amarone the grapes are sourced from several hillsides facing southwest, where they are exposed to the warmer afternoon sun and enjoy the milder climate afforded by the reflection of light from Lake Garda. This is a fruity and approachable wine that lends itself particularly well to matching with food. The Riserva di Costasera is a *cuvée* of the same origins, but with greater tannic structure and deeper color thanks to the small percentage of semi-dried Oseleta that is part of the blend. It's a huge, intense wine with a curiously fresh finish.

To aid drinkers in their choice of wine, Masi has established a vintage classification for Amarone known as the Five Star Rating System that covers the years from the post-war period to the present. At least three stars are required for Amarone Classico Costasera, and a minimum of four out of five for the *cru* wines. Exceptionally good vintages warrant five stars, but when the harvest is poor, meaning that the quality of the grapes is not good enough to justify setting them aside for drying, no Amarone will be made at all. In the past three decades, this was the case in 1982, 1984, 1987, 1992 and 2002. The subtext here is that Amarone made by other wineries in those years should be viewed with caution.

Over the past fifty years, seven vintages have acquired 5-Star status: 1964, 1983, 1988, 1990, 1995, 1997, 2006 and 2007. A Masi Amarone from an exceptionally good vintage does not imply greater expenditure, however, at least not when it leaves the winery. But like all good wines, it does involve other obligations: correct storage, appropriate glassware and the right temperature once poured. Good company is the other prerequisite, of course, but this eludes numerical parameters.

Wine is relatively sensitive to storage conditions, where temperature, light and humidity all play an important role. Too much heat or strong sunlight will cause rapid deterioration, whereas excessive cold could favor osmosis with oxygen through the cork. Between 10 and 18° C (50–64° F) is considered a suitable temperature, bearing in mind that the lower it is the slower the reactions involved in wine maturation are likely to be. Some degree of humidity is also beneficial, because it ensures that the cork does not dry out and allow in oxygen, which would induce spoilage. Very damp cellars bring problems of their own, however, since they tend to cause the evolution of molds on the cork and deterioration of the labels. Ideal ambient humidity is 65–75%, and the rooms used for wine storage should be free of persistent strong smells.

"People often ask why Amarone bottles were traditionally stored upright," Sandro adds. "The reason for this was that in the past, when technology was less advanced, the wine might have had enough residual sugar to bring about further fermentation, which could have blown the cork out. If this happened horizontally, it would have been quite dangerous. Now that we are able to control the sugar situation we can lay the bottles on their sides so that corks are kept damp and elastic."

Tasting

Giorgio Gioco, a revered elderly restaurateur in Verona, declares that the true wine lover should reserve a glass from the second half of a bottle of Amarone for a close friend, whose enjoyment will be even greater the day after the bottle was originally opened. "By then the wine will be at its absolute best, because it will have had time to breathe, and gradually reach the right temperature. A bottle taken from the cellar to the table needs to be acclimatized. It really requires one day for each degree of temperature difference. You can't hurry to open an important bottle of wine."

Granted, this is the pronouncement of a venerable high priest of gastronomic ritual. Not many Amarone drinkers can boast a cellar like that of I 12 Apostoli, Giorgio Gioco's restaurant. Stacked with magnificent bottles, the vaulted underground rooms share one wall with an ancient Roman theater and another with a structure dating back to the 1200s. Yet the essence of Giorgio's conviction is valid for anyone: the temperature at which a wine is served has a profound effect on how it smells and tastes. Getting this wrong can greatly undermine appreciation, especially of a wine as complex as an Amarone. The higher the temperature, the more easily the volatile flavor compounds evaporate, while excessively low temperatures will nullify aromas. The ideal serving temperature for Amarone is 18–19° C (64–66° F), whereas the sweetness of Recioto calls for 14–15° C (57–59° F). An appropriate drinking vessel is also important. Because glass is completely inert, it is potentially ideal for tasting wine. However, it should be immaculately clean, and preferably plain, meaning uncut, unengraved and uncolored. Fine glass is better than chunky, because it allows for closer contact between the palate and the liquid, and stemware avoids the problem of communicating body heat—or indeed scent—to the wine. That said, it is a good idea to avoid strongly perfumed cosmetics when opening a bottle of something special, since they tend to prevail at the expense of what is in the glass.

"For tasting Amarone, an ample tulip-shaped glass is the best," Sandro insists. "It should be filled with no more than two to three fingers of wine, so that the remaining three-quarters of the glass is free to show off the color and cradle the aromas. By swirling the liquid gently against the sides of the glass, an inebriating bouquet is unleashed, enchanting the nose in preparation for the impact of the wine in the mouth. Amarone is a wine to be sipped and savored in a generous mouthful, so that the taste buds are all engaged. Moving it around the mouth will gradually release a complex composition of tastes, ranging from ripe fruit to spices and a hint of chocolate. The impact is extraordinary. It should be swallowed slowly, to appreciate the way the wine regains a certain linearity, with elegant tannins and an extraordinarily long, dry finish featuring a note of bitter almond."

Pairing

While there are no hard and fast rules about what makes a convincing wine and food match, there are certainly two criteria to bear in mind. The match can be based on a contrast in flavors, so that the wine gives the drinker opposite sensations to those of the food. Or the wine can be paired with food on account of its similarities in flavor and in structure. A lighter wine with good acidity can accompany a rich meaty dish, for instance, because it leaves a clean sensation in the mouth that lightens the perception of the food. However, this doesn't always work. To contrast a sweet dessert with a very dry wine would be a mistake. It is much better to match the sweetness of the dish with a likewise sweet wine. As for structure, meaning the type of cooking as well as the quantity and variety of ingredients involved, it is generally true to say that the more elaborate the dish, the more complex the wine needs to be.

In the Valpolicella itself, Amarone relates to food in two distinct ways. There are several local dishes that actually use the wine for cooking. This may sound like rather an extravagant dish, but Masi makes an Amarone specially for culinary preparations that hasn't undergone the usual long aging. Then of course there's the question of exactly which wine best accompanies these slowly cooked, rather wintery dishes. The idea is to create a sort of dialogue between what you're eating and what you're drinking, so the wine needs to have a distinct personality, and at the same time to embody a sort of affability.

"Amarone enriches these dishes with a magnificent range of aromas, fruit, textures and complexity," Sandro declares. "I warmly suggest you take a bottle of the wine home and try out some of the following recipes. They are culinary testimonials that reveal some of the secrets of successful pairing, and reward those who devote a little time to them with a magnificent gastronomic experience. That said, however, I have a simple recipe of my own to offer that doesn't demand much prowess in the kitchen. Take a bite-sized fragment of Parmesan cheese and a teaspoonful of acacia honey, pop them both in your mouth, chew them up to savor the tastes, then take a sip of Amarone and enjoy the ensuing harmonies. Repeat the operation several times, and drink to my health while you're at it."

RAFFAELE AND DEBORAH BOSCAINI—Readers are already acquainted with Raffaele Boscaini, Sandro's son. They know that he heads the Masi technical team, and that he is often abroad appraising the potential for viticulture, or presiding over a tasting of Masi wines. What they are probably unaware of is the fact that both he and his child-psychologist wife, Deborah, are keen cooks who take part in culinary workshops when they have the time, and love to invite friends over for delectable meals in their own home.

Living in a family of winegrowers, Raffaele grew up among people who devoted particular attention to taste. "My mother is an excellent cook, producing creative dishes that often combine something of the culinary traditions of Mantua, where she grew up, with her adopted Venetian cuisine. She always prepared family meals in such an imaginative way that we children got used to a wide range of flavors from an early age," he recalls. "Eating was often a sort of game, and my sisters and I grew up with the idea that you never say 'no' to a dish until you've tried it. I was happy to taste anything new, to experiment with different sensations. My Aunt Elena used to let me 'help' her prepare a variety of simple recipes, which all seemed so special to me. I was always peeping into pots to see what was cooking, and when I was still quite young I was given a boxed set of books, one of recipes and the other on Italian wines. I remember cooking a whole meal for lots of guests with the help of that book—and my mother, of course."

This interest in cooking did not wane with age. Once Raffaele had obtained his driver's license, shopping for food became one of his favorite 'chores.' On holiday with friends he was always cook elect, and when he first met his wife, Deborah, one of the things he found so attractive about her was her delight in tasting different foods.

"We make a point of having proper family meals now that we have children of our own, hoping that they grow up delighting in the magic of taste as well. When we have friends round for a meal, Deborah and I talk about what to serve and prepare it together. Sometimes we don't agree, and what usually happens is I end up in the kitchen and Deborah lays the table and makes it all look incredibly inviting. I travel a lot, and love to try out all kinds of restaurants and national cuisines. Apart from anything else, they're a wonderful source of inspiration for new dishes at home. A great match for the Amarone Mazzano is a fairly traditional dish revisited with a hint of sweetness and spice: beef filet with a mushroom and prune sauce."

SEVERINO BARZAN is the larger-than-life host of La Bottega del Vino, the temple of gastronomy and fine wines in the center of Verona. Under Severino's direction, this historic establishment has built up one of the finest wine lists in Italy, certainly the widest collection of Masi Amarones and Campofiorin to be found anywhere. The Bottega del Vino menu always comprises Veronese classics such as beef braised in Amarone, tripe in broth and Amarone risotto. But for this publication Severino has chosen a recipe that is steeped in history: *Pastisada de caval*, which is horsemeat stew slowly cooked in wine. Many gastronomes would consider this the perfect food match for Amarone.

"According to legend, this dish dates back to the year 489 C.E.," he relates, "when Odoacre, the self-proclaimed sovereign of Italy, and Theodoric, the Ostrogoth king, fought a ferocious battle at the mouth of the Adige Valley, near Verona. By the time they relinquished hostilities, thousands of horses lay slain on the ground, and the starving population ran in to stock up on meat. To preserve it they washed it carefully and left it to marinate for a long time in strong wine, vegetables and herbs, so that it could be cooked as required. The outcome was an unexpectedly generous and delicious dish, the recipe for which has been handed down from one generation to the next, though thankfully we are now able to acquire horsemeat without undergoing bloodthirsty warfare."

Severino Barzan's favorite Amarone to match with the *Pastisada de caval* is the Vaio Armaron Serego Alighieri. Its notes of ripe fruit and spice, with the velvety tannins and elegant finish, marry extraordinarily well with the rich tastiness of the dish.

GABRIELE FERRON loves to quote the old Veronese saying, "*Il riso nasce nell'acqua e muore nel vino,*" which literally means "Rice is born in water and dies in wine," where the rice, far from being moribund, actually undergoes an apotheosis. Gabriele should certainly know. An old friend of Sandro's, with whom he has shared many a wine and food experience across the globe, Gabriele is the person who has saved the age-old rice growing tradition at Isola della Scala, just a few miles south of Verona. Moreover, he has exalted the product, especially the local Vialone Nano variety grown at the family Pila Vecia rice farm, taking it with him on his international travels as risotto ambassador and high priest. He has even taught chefs how to make a proper risotto in China and Japan, where rice was cultivated long before it was introduced to Italy in the fifteenth century.

Gabriele is always experimenting with new risottos, happily trying them out on his guests and carefully pairing them up with Masi wines, from whites such as Masianco to Campofiorin and Amarone. "People always think risotto is a rather antisocial dish, at least for the cook, because they believe it should be stirred during the entire cooking process," he says. "In actual fact it's a simple dish that doesn't demand constant attention as long as you respect two rules: excellent quality rice such as our Vialone Nano, and a quantity of liquid that is twice that of the rice." One of Gabriele's favorites is Risotto with Carp, which has returned to the waterways of his native Isola della Scala since he managed to persuade a collective of local growers to eschew pesticides. However, he also delights in preparing that most classic of local dishes, Risotto with Amarone, which he likes to accompany with the Riserva di Costasera. "Remember to open it well in advance," he adds.

CORRADO BENEDETTI has some enticing and slightly unusual recommendations to make regarding the marriage of wine with food. They are based on the idea that an important wine like Amarone (or indeed Recioto) does not necessarily have to accompany a sophisticated culinary creation, or indeed a dish that has been cooked. It can also complement certain cold cuts and cheeses so perfectly that the two together become in meal in themselves.

The Benedettis have been involved in the preparation of traditional foods for several generations. The business is located at Sant'Anna d'Alfaedo, a small town perched on the slopes of the Lessinia Mountains above the Valpolicella, at an altitude of over 900 meters (3,000 feet). Surrounded by woodland and lush mountain pastures, the area provides excellent grazing for cattle, which is why it is also renowned for its cheeses. The Benedettis originally ran a small dairy, later expanding into pig breeding and the production of preserved meats. When Corrado joined the family firm he decided the time was ripe for expansion and specialization, understanding that there was a market for first class products well beyond the unspoiled hillsides of his hometown. The Benedettis no longer raise their own pigs, but make sure that only the best pork goes into the production of their cold cuts, which are strung up in underground maturing cellars before being hung from the beams of the busy store above. This outlet also entices customers with a magnificent selection of cheeses, largely made in the immediate vicinity and matured by the Benedettis.

Corrado's experience as an *affineur* of fine cheeses has led him to perfect the art of maturing them in a number of different ways: wrapped in walnut leaves, covered with rosemary and sage, and in a variety of grape musts, including that of Amarone. "This is actually a time-honored practice that dates back at least as far as the First World War, if not before," he says. "The story told is that farmers anxious to hide their food stocks from marauding soldiers simply placed whole forms of cheese in a barrel containing grape juice and skins. Whatever its origins, we have perfected the technique by immersing the form in the must obtained from semi-dried grapes for one month, then washing and drying it before vacuum wrapping it to mature for six months to two years. The outcome maintains all the herbal flavors typical of mountain pasture cheeses, but with the addition of greater depth and a certain peppery pungency."

It is easy to imagine spending a memorable evening with a bottle of Amarone and a plate of these Monte Veronese cheeses, to be nibbled in order of ripeness. Corrado would suggest Campofiorin as an ideal match for the smooth consistency and distinct, persistent flavor of the Monte Veronese raw milk cheese that has been cellar aged on wooden racks for twenty-four months. For the cheese known as *Ubriaco all'Amarone* (drunk on Amarone), which has spent at least a month in fresh Corvina, Rondinella and Molinara must before being cellar aged for a further six to eight months, he would choose the great Amarone Riserva di Costasera. It's an ideal encounter, like an amicable meeting between two heads of state who actually agree on everything, from philosophy to policy. But perhaps the most interesting pairing of all involves a creamy, blue-veined cheese called Erborinato Veja, and the Masi Recioto degli Angeli. Here the rounded, fruity aromas of the wine and the gentle pungency of the cheese seem made for each other.

NADIA SANTINI and her husband Antonio preside over one of the high temples of European gastronomy. Far from being located in Paris, Berlin, Milan or Madrid, however, the family restaurant is hidden away in the countryside beside the River Oglio, between the provinces of Mantua and Brescia. Surrounded on all sides by the great plain that stretches out to the horizon, the 3 Michelin star Ristorante Dal Pescatore has become a place of pilgrimage for devotees of fine food from all corners of the globe. It thus seems appropriate that to reach it should require a certain passion, and an unfailing sense of direction.

"For us, welcoming guests and cooking for them is a form of exchange that is spiritually enriching, something we do because we really believe in the value of this most basic form of interaction. That's what partaking of food is really all about," Nadia explains. "It's a form of giving and taking which starts with the gifts of nature, the fish from the river and the vegetables in the garden. What I do is simply transform them with love so that other people can enjoy them too. There's a sort of magic in this translation, which I believe to be the essence of our profession as cooks."

The stretch of water behind the comfortable one-story building which houses the restaurant is rich in fish; not far off is a pond inhabited by ducks, and the surrounding countryside offers a range of game. The menu at Dal Pescatore mirrors the seasons, drawing from the Santini family culinary tradition and enriched with Nadia's inspired approach. "Cuisine is not archeology," she says. "It evolves with man, becoming part of him and adapting to the changing times."

One of the dishes beloved of guests at Dal Pescatore is the breast of duck cooked in balsamic vinegar, with which Antonio Santini warmly recommends a well-aged Campolongo di Torbe Amarone.

Of all food writers, PAOLO ROBERTO is surely the best known worldwide, though probably not in his capacity as a gastronome. Paolo is the real life Italian boxer who features in the second volume of Stieg Larsson's hugely successful fiction narrative, the Millennium Trilogy. He was born in Naples, but moved as a boy with his family to Sweden, where his chosen sport provided him with fulfillment, fame and an alternative to immigrant marginalization.

"I was practically born in the kitchen," he says, "in the sense that I spent my early days surrounded by the smells of olive oil, garlic, oregano, tomato sauce and the other ingredients typical of Neapolitan cuisine. These weren't easy to come by in Sweden in those days, but every weekend my parents would seek them out to create meals that were a way of keeping in touch with our origins and culture. Food was part of our identity, a relationship with where we came from."

When Paolo gave up boxing, he started to gather together some of the family stories that his aunties back in Naples loved to relate. "Many of them revolved around food, and this gave me the idea of collecting up the recipes and describing the meals and their tastes and smells so that my children Enzo and Elisa, who were born in Sweden, would know about their roots. It must have hit a note with other people too, because I've sold over 200,000 copies."

When friends and family from Naples visit Paolo in Sweden, he loves to shock them by pairing the Costasera Amarone Masi with a classic Neapolitan pasta dish served with a meat sauce. "Initially they are thrown off balance because they don't know the wine, and imagine it to be something far too heavy and sophisticated for their tastes. I love to watch the surprise on their faces when they try it, and realize how approachable it is. In my view, it's the wine of welcome. Amarone is the heart of hospitality."

One feature that PIERO SELVAGGIO shares with Paolo Roberto is the sort of displacement that can give rise to a confident synthesis of different traditions. Piero's hometown is Modica in southeast Sicily, where much of his family still resides, a town with a fine tradition of gastronomy surrounded by some of the island's most prestigious winegrowing. Piero left Sicily for the United Staters when he was eighteen, working as a dishwasher and a chauffeur for many years before finally opening the Valentino restaurant in Santa Monica, Los Angeles, in 1972. Today he is considered by both his peers and his many faithful customers as one of the finest restaurateurs in the United States.

"I've always believed in Amarone. It's a unique wine, with such a wealth of aromas and complex tastes. Right from the outset I've made sure our cellar was stocked with some of the best vintages of premium Amarone producers, along with bottles of Barolo, Brunello and some Taurasi. In America, diners initially found Amarone to be slightly difficult, probably because no one had explained just why it was different, and people's palates were attuned to little beyond Cabernet, Merlot and Pinot Noir. Now things have improved enormously, not least because in general sommeliers are better informed. I love to suggest an Amarone to accompany the entire meal, on occasion even with a spicy seafood pasta dish to start off with. But it's a wine that also pairs magnificently with buffalo meat and pork pricked with cloves, served with spiced greens and a conserve of apple or onion."

When he entertains friends at home, Piero loves to marinate lamb or game sausages in Amarone, then barbecue them and serve them with creamy polenta. "For a meal like this I would choose the Vaio Armaron Amarone Serego Alighieri," he explains. "It has magnificent body and a hint of spice alongside the ripe fruit that I find irresistible. I love the way the dry, elegant finish remains in the mouth, like a lovely strain of music on the ear. It also pairs perfectly with one of our signature dishes at the Valentino restaurant: Lamb with almonds, walnuts and pine nuts."

The complexity of Amarone lies to a large extent in the balance between the initial perception of sweetness, the fullness of the fruit and the distinctly spicy notes. Perhaps it is these features in such perfect equilibrium that account for the wine's remarkable success in Asia. It seems to pair up naturally well with a number of dishes that have little in common with the western culinary tradition, as Alessandra Boscaini, Sandro's younger daughter, has discovered on her travels to distant destinations. "I handle much of the business side for the non-European markets, and was never particularly surprised to find that our wines went down well with Russian gourmets," she declares. "But what did initially astonish me was how readily the Japanese have taken to Amarone, and how they love to pair it with certain dishes typical of their cuisine. I have to admit that the outcome of these slightly unorthodox pairings is always completely convincing."

One of the greater arbitrators of these "mixed marriages" is Japanese sommelier Kazuo Naito, who in 2007 won the national Jet Cup award for Japanese experts in Italian wines, organized by the Japan Europe Trading organization, the Japan Sommelier Association and the Italian Institute of Culture in Tokyo.

"Here in Japan we are very fond of tasty soy sauces for marinating ingredients and using as a condiment," Naito explains. "For instance, *Tori no Teriyaki*, which is chicken marinated in a sweet soy sauce, and then broiled. Amarone pairs with this dish magnificently. Another perfect match is with eel, which we like to prepare in various ways. *Anago no Nitsume* is stewed eel served with a sweet soy sauce, often accompanied by a little *wasabi*, to refresh the palate. The fullness of the Masi Amarones, and their dry, soft finish, also go well with another typical Japanese dish that is quite rich and slightly bitter: *Tori liver shouyu-ni*, or spiced chicken livers stewed in soy sauce."

VII

DINNER WITH AMARONE: RECIPES

DEBORAH AND RAFFAELE BOSCAINI match MAZZANO AMARONE with

Beef filet with a mushroom and prune sauce

Ingredients for 4 people:
4 thick slices of beef filet (3 cm/1.3 inch)
400 gr (14 oz) fresh mushrooms (champignons, porcini,
    honey mushrooms)
80 gr (3 oz) pitted prunes
half an onion
1 cinnamon stick
oil
butter
salt and pepper

Finely chop the onion and sauté it in oil, then add the diced mushrooms. Salt and pepper to taste, and cook for around 40 minutes, until the liquid from the mushrooms has evaporated. Add the diced prunes and the whole cinnamon stick. Cook for a further 20 minutes on a low flame. Remove the cinnamon stick.

Take the beef filets, tie them around their circumference so that they don't lose their shape during cooking, then cook them for 3 minutes on each side in the pan where you have already melted a knob of butter and a spoonful of oil. Salt them and place them on a warm serving dish, covering them with the mushroom sauce.

SEVERINO BARZAN of the BOTTEGA DEL VINO in Verona would suggest VAIO ARMARON SEREGO ALIGHIERI to accompany the historic recipe for

Pastisada de caval

Ingredients for 4 people:

750 gr (26 oz) horse meat
500 gr (18 oz) ripe tomatoes
30 gr (1 oz) butter
1 large onion, 1 stick of celery, 1 carrot
3 spoonfuls of extra virgin olive oil
5 dl (2 cups) of Amarone
salt and pepper

Place the meat in a casserole and let it marinate for 12 hours with half of the Amarone and the chopped onion, carrot and celery. In another terracotta pot, melt the butter with three spoonfuls of olive oil, and cook the chopped up vegetables from the marinade. Add the skinned and diced tomatoes and cook on a medium flame for 15 minutes, then pour in the rest of the Amarone and cook on a low flame for a further three hours.

Pass the gravy through a sieve and serve with the meat, accompanied by fresh or grilled polenta.

GABRIELE FERRON of the RISERIA FERRON rice farm at Isola della Scala, near Verona, loves to serve RISERVA DI COSTASERA with his

Risotto all'Amarone

Ingredients for 4 people

400 gr (14 oz) semifino Vialone Nano rice
400 gr (14 oz) vegetable broth
1 medium sized red onion

400 gr (14 oz) Masi Amarone wine
2 tablespoons extra-virgin olive oil
2 tablespoons butter
100 gr (3.5 oz) Grana cheese, grated
nutmeg, chili pepper flakes

Sauté the onion together with a little bit of chili pepper flakes in some extra virgin olive oil. Remove the chili flakes. Add the rice and toast it in some olive oil for 2–3 minutes. Add the Amarone, previously heated, and the warm vegetable broth. Stir gently, lower the flame and cover. Remove from heat after 16–17 minutes. Add the butter, some grated nutmeg and the cheese. Stir once more gently and serve.

NADIA SANTINI of the RISTORANTE DAL PESCATORE at Canneto dull'Oglio, near Mantua, pairs CAMPOLOGO DI TORBE AMARONE with her

Breast of duck cooked in traditional Modena balsamic vinegar and served with fruit mustard

Ingredients for 4 people
2 duck breasts
80 gr (3 oz) butter
juice of 1 lemon
2 spoonfuls of cognac
40 gr (1.5 oz) red wine
40 gr (1.5 oz) white wine
2 dl (7 oz.) meat broth
sage, rosemary, pepper, salt
traditional Modena balsamic vinegar

Salt and pepper the two duck breasts. Melt the butter in an aluminum pan, and when it begins to brown place the duck breasts in it skin-side down. When they have turned golden, flip them over and brown the other side so that all the flavors are preserved. Splash them with the white wine, followed by the cognac and then the lemon juice. Add the herbs, and keep cooking on a medium flame while the liquid reduces. Remove the breasts, put them on a baking tray and place them in the oven at 150°C (300°F). To finish the sauce, add the red wine and the meat broth and cook until reduced to the desired density. At the last minute, add the balsamic vinegar.

Prepare the serving dish by placing the fruit mustard to one side, then adding the sauce with the two duck breasts taken off the bone.

PAOLO ROBERTO, television gastronaut and author with real punch, chooses COSTASERA AMARONE to go with his

Pasta Naples style, with chops, meatballs and sausage

Ingredients for 4–6 people

600–800 gr (20–28 oz) short pasta, such as rigatoni or ziti

for the meat:

600 gr (20 oz) veal shoulder

500 gr (18 oz) pork ribs

250 gr (9 oz) Italian sausage

75 gr (2–3 oz) bacon in 15x18 cm rashers (6x7inches)

1 finely diced garlic clove

chopped parsley

2 tbsp extra virgin olive oil

a pinch of salt

ground pepper

for the sauce:

700 gr (23 oz.)tomato sauce

375 gr (14 oz.)chopped tomatoes

1 yellow onion

1 dl (7 tablespoons) extra virgin olive oil

a pinch of salt

a pinch of sugar

0.15 dl (1 tablespoon) red wine

for the meatballs:
250 gr (9 oz) mixed minced meat
75 gr (2–3 oz) stale bread
1 egg
0.5 dl (3½ tablespoons) parmesan
3 tbsp parsley
1 tbsp extra virgin olive oil
salt and pepper to taste
2 dl (7 oz.) sunflower oil for frying

Cut the veal down the middle without separating the two parts, then open it up and beat it flat, salt and pepper it, then roll it up and fasten it with string. Salt and pepper the bacon, then roll it up and tie it. Heat the oil in a large casserole and soften the diced onion in it, adding the wine and letting it boil for 5–10 minutes. Add the tomato, sugar and salt, and cook the meat on a low flame with the top on for one and a half hours. Add salt and pepper. Once it has finished cooking, the meat should be very soft. Add the sausages around 30 minutes before the end. In the meantime, prepare the meatballs. Soak the stale bread in water for a few minutes, then squeeze it out and crumble it, mixing it with the other ingredients: minced meat, egg, parmesan, parsley, oil, salt and pepper. Form meatballs and fry them in hot oil for 5–10 minutes. Around 10 minutes before the ragout is ready, add it to the meat and the tomato sauce.

Lastly, remove the meat and serve it cut into slices with the well-drained pasta, cooked *al dente*, and topped with the sauce.

PIERO SELVAGGIO of the RISTORANTE VALENTINO in Las Vegas, USA, suggests VAIO ARMARON SEREGO ALIGHIERI as the ideal match for his

Lamb with almonds, walnuts and pine nuts
Ingredients for 4 people
½ cup (4 oz) butter

½ cup unblanched almonds, sliced
½ cup walnuts, coarsely chopped
½ cup pine nuts
1 cup bread crumbs, finely ground
12 single-rib lamb chops, trimmed and bones scraped
      (French style)
2–3 tbsp all-purpose flour
4 large eggs, beaten
salt and pepper, to taste

For the salad
12 ounces mixed baby greens
¼ cup fresh mint, finely chopped
¼ cup fresh basil, finely chopped
½ cup citrus vinaigrette

Clarify the butter by melting it over low heat in a small, heavy-duty saucepan. Let it cool, then skim the foam off and pour the clarified butter into a cup, discarding the solids at the bottom of the pan.

In a food processor fitted with the metal blade, pulse to combine the almonds, walnuts, pine nuts and bread crumbs. Transfer to shallow bowl.

Pat the lamb chops dry and dredge the meat lightly in flour. Dip them in the beaten eggs, allowing the excess to drip back into the bowl. Coat them completely with the nut mixture and set aside.

In a large, non-stick skillet, heat a few tablespoons of the clarified butter over medium heat. Cook the lamb chops 2–3 minutes per side for medium-rare. Remove from the skillet and drain on paper towels. Season with salt and pepper and arrange 3 chops on each plate.

In a large bowl, toss together the greens, mint, basil and citrus vinaigrette. Serve the salad on the side with the chops.

EPILOGUE

Sandro Boscaini likes to describe Amarone as the Marco Polo of wines—in other words, a wine that travels, proud of its own heritage, but not opposed to diversity. However, the testimonials above suggest that the expression implies rather more than the wine's ability to represent the Veneto, its history and some of its finest landscape. What is it exactly that makes Amarone so readily embraceable by countries and cultures far removed from its origins in a small corner of northeast Italy? Arguably the fact that it embodies a trait characteristic of all successful travelers: the ability to be personable, to be perceived as particular and enchanting in different ways by different people.

It's a question of first impressions. That first sip of Amarone is uniquely engaging: warm but never cloying; inviting but not invasive; generous without prodigality; and distinguished in a way that never suggests hauteur. But it also has to do with secondary sensations and reflections. The initial illusion of sweetness gives way immediately to a depth of flavors that is both delectable and fascinating. How is it that a wine can be at the same time so open to encounter, and yet profound?

Perhaps the answer to this question lies in the original anthropocentric analogy. Every now and then life offers unforgettable encounters. Sometimes this comes under the heading of love at first sight, though the duration factor of such meetings is probably not very high. More often, encountering someone who makes a lasting impact involves the mind as much as it does the senses. It's a matter of balance, and the perception that immediate attraction, far from implying superficiality, is actually an invitation to further exchange and discovery. Such people may not be numerous, but they exist. Generally they are quietly communicative, learned but never pedantic, and generous without wishing to influence or belittle whoever is on the receiving end.

What provides a human being with such gifts? The right balance of nature and nurture, with an emphasis on the education that begins at home. And so it is with Amarone. Nature has provided all the ingredients, but they would be nothing, or very little, without the wisdom and expertise of grape growers and winemakers. In the case of this particular wine, the "education" can be traced back to the distant past, when man began selecting what he grew, and processing what he harvested. In more recent times, seven generations of the Boscaini family have made their contribution to the development and character of the wine by working with admirable coherence and foresight in the pursuit of quality. But it is Sandro who has created the conditions for the renaissance of a modern wine with an ancient heart. When Australian wine critic Bruce Schoenfeld pointed out that Sandro "is to Amarone what Angelo Gaja is to Barbaresco and Piero Antinori to Chianti,"[1] he was not only illustrating the way the best of modernity embodies history, but also the fact that only a creative individual can bring these elements to fruition.

To accomplish this, Sandro has avoided the role of the protagonist, quietly operating so that a whole extended team of collaborators could contribute their expertise to the collective effort. Natural curiosity, great rigor and a quiet sense of humor underlie an achievement that has required uncommon vision, patience, perseverance and faith in others as well as the wine. A Masi Amarone speaks for itself with consummate eloquence. This book merely hopes to have portrayed the man who gave the wine its wonderful voice.

---

1 Bruce Schoenfeld, *Saveur*, 14.

APPENDIXES

I

GRAPE VARIETIES

he Venetian regions in general, and Verona in particular, boast a singularly rich heritage of grape varieties. In the course of time, however, only three of these have come to play a major role in the wines most characteristic of the Valpolicella: Corvina, Rondinella and Molinara.

The Corvina variety, which accounts for 70–75% of the blend in the Masi Amarones, invests the wine with good structure and slightly herbaceous notes not found in the other members of the classic trio. During appassimento these grapes are subject to *Botrytis* (noble rot), which produces high levels of glycerol and gluconic acid, thereby contributing to the wine's body, intensity and smoothness. The Rondinella variety is productive, consistent and resistant to blight, which for many years made it particularly popular. It confers color and tannins to the final product, along with levels of glycerol that are proportionally high in relation to the grape's relative resistance to *Botryitis*. It holds a precious 20–25% stake in four of the five Masi Amarones. Molinara, the third variety, cannot lay claim to much body and color, but does have good acidity, which contributes to the drinkability and spice tones of Amarone, an important feature in wines made from grapes with high sugar concentrations.

In recent years, however, a fourth variety has come to the fore, thanks to Masi's farsighted experimental vineyard in which forty-eight forgotten varieties have been rescued, replanted and put to the test. This is Oseleta, a small grape with relatively large pips that is not prolific in the vineyard and produces a good thirty percent less juice than other varieties when crushed. The skins are thick and dark, however, investing the wine with plenty of color and berry aromas, while the pips, when fully ripe, provide very pleasant tannins.

Masi currently produces a Corvina and Oseleta blend called "Toar," which marries the value of indigenous grapes with the stature of the finest international wines; and the Oseleta varietal labeled "Osar," featuring great structure, depth and complexity, as well as impressive aging potential. Since Oseleta has also proved to be very promising when semi-dried, around ten percent is now added to the Costasera Riserva, Masi's most recent Amarone, a wine of such character, fine tannic structure and exceptional color that it can hold its own in company with the great reds of the world.

II

APPASSIMENTO

ppassimento is the process of partially drying grapes in order to obtain a greater concentration of color, flavors and aromas in the wine made from them. Because partially dried grapes also have a greater concentration of sugars, the process is often used to produce sweet or highly concentrated wines. In the Venetian regions, however, where the technique dates back to Roman times, appassimento has long been used to produce dry wines as well. These tend to be full-bodied, complex and relatively high in alcohol. Entirely made of grapes that are semi-dried over a period of four months, Amarone is the supreme expression of the genre, while Recioto is its traditional sweet counterpart.

The grapes suitable for appassimento must be perfectly healthy, and not too tightly bunched together. After harvesting, they are laid out to rest on bamboo racks in special drying rooms known as *fruttai* for around four months, during which time they lose thirty to forty percent of their original weight. Certain grape varieties are subject to *Botrytis*, the benevolent mold known as "noble rot" that will invest the future wine with velvety smoothness, rounded body and distinctly spicy notes. Of the three varieties that traditionally go into Amarone, Corvina is particularly susceptible to *Botrytis* during appassimento. The semi-dried grapes are generally pressed between late January and early February. In the case of Amarone, the maceration and fermentation processes continue for forty-five to fifty days, and are followed by at least three years aging in wood before bottling.

Masi's expertise with this production method has led it to experiment with partially-dried grapes from its Castions di Strada estate, in the Friuli region north east of the Valpolicella. By semi-drying the native Refosco grapes along with some Carmenère for around fifty days, the winery has produced the innovative and majestic Grandarella red. Moreover, it has exported the technique to the province of Mendoza in Argentina, where it produces Corbec, a blend of slightly dried Corvina and Malbec, and Passo Doble, which marries fresh Malbec with semi-dried Corvina.

When appassimento is used in conjunction with wine made from fresh grapes, the outcome is depth and complexity blended with freshness. The technique for achieving this desirable goal was pioneered by Masi in its groundbreaking Campofiorin, which first appeared on the market in 1964. It was initially made by refermenting the fresh Valpolicella red on the lees of Amarone. The Boscaini family registered the term "Ripasso" to refer to this system, later donating the trademark to the Verona Chamber of Commerce. While many other Valpolicella wineries now offer their own version of Ripasso, today Masi makes Campofiorin by adding a certain percentage of partially dried grapes to a wine made from fresh grapes so that it undergoes a second fermentation. The outcome is a wine endowed with much richer color, aroma and taste, with elegant, slightly sweet tannins.

Masi has also applied a similar process to produce wines such as Brolo di Campofiorin, which is a special selection of Campofiorin, and the Valpolicella Classico Anniversario Serego Alighieri. The winery also uses appassimento to make a white wine, Masianco, a blend of fresh Pinot Grigio with wine from semi-dried Verduzzo grapes from the Friuli vineyards. In all likelihood, appassimento will play a role in several other persuasive Masi wines in coming years.

III

MASI TECHNICAL GROUP

At many wineries, the person invested with most decision-making regarding what wines are made, and how, is the enologist. Be this the in-house expert or an itinerant consultant, the winemaker takes on great responsibility almost single-handed. Because no one is infallible, however, this widespread approach can be risky. Furthermore, it is also inevitably one-sided, since the pronouncements of one individual are unlikely to take into account all the perspectives that a group decision could bring into play.

Masi has always preferred teamwork, seeing in it a form of enrichment that will benefit both wine production as such, and the positioning of the wines on the market. To this end in the mid-1980s it formed the Gruppo Tecnico Masi, known under the acronym GTM, coordinated by consultant biotechnologist Lanfranco Paronetto, one of the country's foremost experts in yeasts. The idea was to create a team devoted to a program of quality control and ongoing research through regular meetings, tasting sessions, technical analyses, and monitored experimentation and appraisal. Since its inception, it has grown to include Raffaele Boscaini, the GTM general manager; Sandro Boscaini, responsible for overall strategy; Lucio Brancadoro, who teaches at the Faculty of Agriculture at Milan University; the agronomist Cesare Marcazzan; the enologists Roberto Tebaldi and Dante Cavazzani; their coordinator Andrea Dal Cin; plus Vittorio Zandonà, Barbara Masello and Andrea Farinazzo, the winery's quality control laboratory technicians.

Masi's marketing manager, Luc Descroches, is also an active member of the GTM, as are various consultants for geology and meteorology, as well as other experts from the worlds of dining, distribution and the press.

One of the GTM's major achievements has been the recovery of many forgotten grape varieties that are part of the Venetian viticultural and enological heritage. It has created an experimental vineyard planted with secondary Veronese grape varieties such as Oseleta, Dindarella, Croatina, Negrara and Forsellina. Moreover, its extensive research into grape drying has resulted in the development of the innovative NASA system (Natural Serego Super Assisted) within the drying loft at Gargagnago.

The GTM is also engaged in a specific project designed to enhance the elements that make for typicality in a wine. Particular attention is being paid to the maceration and fermentation stages of the process, with an emphasis on the role of yeasts. The GTM hosts scientific seminars relating to its core interests at Vinitaly, the annual wine fair in Verona, and has published a number of handsome volumes illustrating its endeavors.

The GTM meetings often take place around a long table in the barrel-vaulted ex-cellars of the Valgatara winery. Chaired by Raffaele, the GTM comparative tastings are usually blind, and the participants' written comments are voiced clockwise and logged into the computer, where they become part of a multi-faceted data base essential to further policy making. These events are absolutely serious in terms of content, yet pleasantly light-hearted in tone.

During the past four years, the GTM has also activated the "Quality Grapes Project," with the aim of improving control of all aspects of grape growing. It directly involves all the Masi growers, ensuring them a just financial return for their labors in the pursuit of premium grape production.

For the past four years, the GTM has issued a weekly "Grape-grower's bulletin," providing timely information on weather conditions, the requisite vine treatments, deadlines and legislation regarding grape production, and related activities in both the vineyard and the winery, including harvesting and appassimento. The Masi technicians also regularly visit all the vineyards to check on how the Bulletin instructions are actually working out. The growers are advised on replanting vines, on choice of variety, clone and rootstock, and on the purchase of machinery and equipment. Such visits are also an opportunity for keeping the growers up to date on commercial relations with nurseries and the wine market, for planning participation in wine fairs and conferences, and for directly involving the people who produce the grapes in the annual harvest thanksgiving festival.

IV

YEAST

For millennia the fermentation of grape juice, like the leavening of bread, was deemed a mysterious process. Ritual value was attached to the miraculous production of inebriating liquid from fruit, or the wondrous growth of kneaded dough. Hence the numerous myths, parables and folk tales that revolve around libation and the breaking of bread. They have much in common. Both imply cohesive social interaction, often a form of initiation. And both depend on yeast to be effective.

Because yeasts consist of a single cell, they belong to the lowest ranks of the vegetable kingdom. Yet they undertake some noble operations, which modern microbiology is at last able to explain. The airborne *Saccharomyces cerevisiae*, or yeast involved in making wine (and beer) and in getting bread to rise, are naturally present in many vineyards and established cellars. However, they flourish alongside a great many different strains of ambient yeasts, not all of which will necessarily contribute to the desired fermentation process. Indeed, some of them could throw the good yeasts off course. So modern science has developed cultured yeasts, which are performance geared. In other words, cultured yeasts prevail over the ambient yeasts, and effect the transformations that their indigenous counterparts would accomplish in ideal conditions; that is, consume the sugar present in the grape juice, and emit alcohol and carbon dioxide as by-products of this reaction.

In reality, this process can be hampered by a number of factors. Not all ambient yeasts fare well in high alcohol concentrations. Others cannot tolerate extremes of temperature. In the case of wines obtained through appassimento, for example, there are two potential hurdles. For sweet wines made in the autumn when the sun is still warm, the dried grapes will have sugar concentrations that not all yeasts will be able to cope with. It's a question of balance, the aim being to stop fermentation before all the sugars are transformed into alcohol. With dry wines such as Amarone, on the other hand, the fermentation process takes place in winter, when outside temperatures hover around freezing. Here the difficulty lies in ensuring that the yeasts are able to operate at relatively low temperatures so that fermentation is consistent and not overly protracted.

In the past, producers of Amarone found that fermentation with ambient yeasts went in fits and starts, and took several months to complete. As a result, the wine was unbalanced, revealing flaws that only very long aging in wood could mitigate.

The Masi technical team, in collaboration with the University of Verona, has analyzed this problem in depth, paying special attention to a series of secondary substances produced during fermentation that contribute to the taste and aroma of the wine. They finally opted for the addition of a particular strain of cultured yeast, developed from those found in the drying loft at Gargagnago, that not only operated in the given conditions, but also enhanced particular characteristics that could be described as typical of the "house style."

Apart from making alcohol, the yeasts also protect the nascent wine from oxidation, which is damage caused by contact with oxygen. During fermentation the carbon dioxide produced creates a blanket that prevents such spoilage.

Like all living organisms, yeasts live, labor and die. Once they have converted all of the sugar, they fall to the bottom of the container, where they form a fine sediment known as lees. The lees actually contain certain proteins that offer further enhancement to the wine, which is why superior reds and whites made for aging are often left on their lees for periods that may range from several weeks to a year. But that is another story.

V

MOLDS

ome wines present an unpleasant moldy smell on the nose that is usually perceptible in the mouth as well. This is due to spoilage brought about by the growth of minute fungi on grapes or winery equipment. Many different types of mold can grow on grapes in the vineyard, depending on region and climate. But they are also inclined to prosper in empty barrels and casks, where the spores easily become so embedded in the pores of the wood that they are hard to remove completely. Wine drinkers are also familiar with the sort of mold that taints corks, imbuing the wine with such an unattractive smell that it cannot be drunk. This is due to a chemical reaction between the chlorine solution used for bleaching cork and the endemic molds present in the material.

Many of the important fungal diseases that threaten the vineyard originated in America and caused tremendous damage in Europe when they were inadvertently introduced during the mid- to late-nineteenth century, because the European *Vitis vinifera* species was not resistant to them. The earliest remedy was a mixture of lime, copper sulfate and water, first recorded in 1885 and known as the 'Bordeaux mixture.' Today, there is a wide range of agricultural chemicals to control undesirable molds.

Not all molds are unwelcome, however. The strain called *Botrytis*, which attacks grape bunches, can take the form of a feared gray rot (*Botrytis cinerea*) which appears in vineyards in damp climates, or when there is severe rainfall near harvest, because the spores germinate on wet surfaces and in high ambient humidity. When morning mists are followed by warm, sunny afternoons, on the other hand, a benevolent form of *Botrytis*, known as noble rot, will make an important contribution to the quality of the white grapes used for sweet wines. This it does by penetrating the skins of the ripe fruit with filaments that leave minute brown spots on the skin, making it unassailable by other harmful micro-organisms. The mold aids desiccation on the vine, turning the grapes golden, then pink or purple, and brown, often with an ash-like powder on the surface. Because this form of *Botrytis* consumes the acids in the grapes faster than it does the sugars, the overall effect in the wine is greater sugar concentration and a velvety quality produced by glycerol and gluconic acid.

In the drying rooms of the Valpolicella, *Botrytis* can also contribute to the excellence and style of Amarone. A greater degree of *Botrytis*, and thus of glycerol, will make the wine more fiery, rounded, velvety and full-bodied, with intense aromas of overripe fruit or fruit preserved in spirit. Less or no *Botrytis* will produce more austere wines with greater tannic structure.

VI

FIVE STAR RATING SYSTEM

uring the 1970s, when Masi was devoting great energy to reforming the quality and image of Verona's classic wines, it became clear that fundamental improvements in vineyard and cellar techniques should be accompanied by a new marketing and communication philosophy. Among other things, this meant approaching wine selection from the consumer's point of view.

One of the first issues to address was how to help choose a particular wine and vintage, given the anomalous nature of Amarone with respect to other Venetian and Italian wines. In the case of Amarone, it is not sufficient to have high quality grapes at harvest, because the climate also has to be ideal during the long drying period. This means a wide temperature range, a dry, breezy climate, not too many warm, humid days, and the absence of fog. Only when conditions are optimal both at harvest and during appassimento will the Amarone be at its best.

The Five Star Rating System is a specially devised vintage classification for Amarone that takes into consideration not only climate conditions from spring vegetation through to the grape harvest, but also the behavior of the grapes during the drying process, and the subsequent evolution of the wine from fermentation through to aging. While exceptionally good vintages warrant five stars, at least three stars are required for Amarone Classico Costasera, and at least four out of five for the cru wines. When the harvest is deemed too poor, meaning that the quality of the grapes is not good enough to justify setting them aside for drying, or the drying process itself is compromised by unhelpful weather, no Amarone will be made at all. This was the case in 1982, 1984, 1987, 1992 and 2002. Only a limited selection will be singled out for drying when prevailing conditions have been average. For an exceptional vintage, on the other hand, between thirty and sixty percent of the harvest will undergo appassimento and be used for Amarone.

The Five Star Rating System covers vintages from the end of World War II to the present. During this half-century, seven vintages have been classified as 5-Star, and are marked as such on the bottle label: 1964, 1983, 1988, 1990, 1995, 1997, 2006 and 2007. What this implies for the consumer is not only a wine of particular excellence, but also one that will continue to evolve in the bottle over many years of cellar maturation, during which different characteristics will come to the fore. The Amarone from an exceptionally good vintage does not carry a higher price tag, however, at least not when it leaves the Masi estate. The aim is simply to provide consumers with an objective scale of appraisal which will help them understand what to buy and when, and how long to keep it before enjoying it with friends.